JN033559

Grammar-based English Practice
for College Students

# 文法活用の
# 大学英語演習

八木克正 [監修]

井上亜依・住吉誠・藏薗和也 [著]

開拓社

# はしがき

　本書は，2021 年に上梓された『現代高等英文法：学習文法から科学文法へ』（八木克正著，開拓社，以後『現代高等英文法』）のテキストブック版です．このテキストブックは，『現代高等英文法』を簡潔に説明し，その内容を正しく理解できているかどうかを練習問題ではかるという「受信」した知識を「発信」で確認することに重きを置いています．

　日本の英語教育は，大学入学試験のための英文法がすべてであり，それが不変のように考えられています．しかし英語という言語は，世界中で広範囲にわたって使用される言語の 1 つであり，時々刻々と変化をしています．そのような変化を余すところなく説明する役割を辞書が担っていますが，高等英文法に特化し，英語の変化を詳述した著書や参考書は寡聞にして知りません．このような状況のもと，この『現代高等英文法』は現代英語のありのままの姿や変化を忠実に記述し，それらに説明を与えた文法書です．

　本書は，『現代高等英文法』を正しく理解し，発信することを目的としています．この目的達成のために，本書には次の特徴があります．1 つ目は，広くすべての事象に適応することができる文法規則を，日本人英語学習者にわかりやすく説明しました．2 つ目は，効果的な発信のために，本書の説明を正しく理解できているかどうかをはかる練習問題を設けました．3 つ目は，本書の内容をさらに深掘りして学びたい方に，『現代高等英文法』との cross reference（相互参照）ができるようになっています．この 3 点により，読者の方々が確実に高等英文法を理解し，活用することに役立つと信じています．

　では，なぜ本書のような「高等英文法の受信および発信」に重きを置いた教材が必要なのでしょうか．それは，「あらゆる場面で使用される英語を正しく理解し，伝わる英語および通じる英語の習得のため」です．ご存じかもしれませんが，日本人英語学習者（高等英文法を学習するレベルの人たち）の英語力は決して高いものではありません．具体的に述べると，CEFR (Common European Framework of Reference for Languages: Learning, teaching, assessment, ヨーロッパ言語共通参照枠）によると，日本人英語学習者の約 8 割が 3 段階のレベル（Level A（a basic user），Level B（an independent user），Level C（a proficient user））のうち Level A に該当する，という研究結果が報告されています．また，テストの妥当性はどうであれ，2021 年に発表されたある英語実力テストを受けた日本人（任意による受験です）の英語力は「低い」に位置づけられています．また，昨今の大学受験生の英語力は教育制度の影響により，リスニング力とスピーキング力は昔より向上している，と言われています．一方，リーディング力とライティング力は低下している，とも言われています．いずれにせよ，受信・発信とともに，日本での英語学習者はこれまで培った英語力をうまく活用できていない印象を受けます．このような事実は，とても残念なことです．

またこの事実は，昨今の日本人英語学習者が情報収集のために頼りにしている Social Networking Service（SNS）等の英語で書かれた情報を正しく受信し，それに対して自己の意見を述べることの難しさにも影響を与えています．その困難を克服するために，学習者が頼りにしている翻訳機能ソフトがありますが，仮にその翻訳機能を利用して自己の意見を述べたとしても，残念ながら，どことなくぎこちなく英語らしさに欠けていることがあります．

本書は，半期 15 回の授業で終了することができるよう 15 章から成り立っています．もしくは，通年 30 回で本書を詳しく時間をかけて学習することも可能です．各章が終わった後，練習問題を解き，本書の内容をどれほど理解しているか確認をしてください．授業以外に独学で勉強している際に，英字新聞などで疑問に感じる英文や理解が難しい英文があれば本書を辞書のように活用し，そのような英文を正しく理解し，発信できるよう努めてください．

本書は，日本での英語学習者に大学入学試験を受けるまでの英語がすべてではないこと，英語は変化すること，自身の力で英語を理解し発信すること，この 3 点を達成してもらうために高等英文法の実態を丁寧に説明しています．本書が現代英語の受信及び発信の一助になることを著者一同，切望します．

本書は，次に述べる方々のご尽力なしに作成することはできませんでした．出

縄貴良氏と今佑介氏には，細部に至るまで原稿を確認していただき，貴重なコメントを頂いたことに感謝申し上げます．また，開拓社出版部の川田賢氏には万事お力添えを賜りましたこと，衷心より御礼申し上げます．

2022 年　著者を代表して　井上亜依

# 目　次

## PART I　文と文型

## PART II　述語動詞構成要素と準動詞

viii

## PART III　品詞を中心として

# Table, Figure 一覧

## 本書で使用した略語一覧

S   subject（主語）

V   predicative verb（述語動詞）

C   complement（補語）

O   object（目的語）

A   adverbial（副詞的語句）

N.   noun（名詞）

Pron.   pronoun（代名詞）

PP   part participle（過去分詞）

ART.   article（冠詞）

V   verb（動詞）

AUX   auxiliary verb（助動詞）

Adj.   adjective（形容詞）

Adv.   adverb（副詞）

Prep.   preposition（前置詞）

Conj.   conjunction（接続詞）

Intr.   interjection（間投詞）

NP   noun phrase（名詞句）

that   that 節

to do   to 不定詞

PrepP.   Prepositional Phrase（前置詞句）

## ■本書の使い方

本書で学習する前に，下記の点に留意してください．

＊用例は『現代高等英文法』と同じであるため，日本語訳は割愛しています．
日本語訳がある英文は，本書独自の英文であることを示します．

＊本文中に出てくる用語や略語は，「用語・略語の説明」にすべて記載しています．

＊本書の内容について深掘りして学習したい方に，＜もっと詳しく＞というセクションがあります．本書の拠り所となった『現代高等英文法』のページ数を記載していますので，そのページを読んで知識を蓄えてください．

1. 各章を熟読し，理解したことを日本語で説明できるようにしてください．本書をさらに深く勉強したい方は，『現代高等英文法』を参照してください．参照ページは，各章のタイトルのところに記してあります．
2. 各章の最後にある練習問題を解いてください．
3. 練習問題はインストラクションに従い，英語で言えると同時に英文を書くことができるようになってください．
4. 3. の後，練習問題の答えの英文を和訳できるようにしてください．

この 1. ～ 4. を繰り返し行うことを，お勧めします．

### 〈授業計画案〉

15 回の授業で本書を終える場合の計画案です．通年 30 回の授業で本書を使用する場合は，各週の勉強内容に 2 週かけることも一案です．練習問題は，授業中に理解度を測るために活用できますが，宿題として受講生に取り組んでもらうことも可能です．

第 1 週　授業説明，本書の説明，PART I 第 1 章　文，文型，文を構成する基本要素
第 2 週　PART I 第 2 章　修飾要素，独立要素，文の種類

xviii

# 文と文型

# 第1章 文，文型，文を構成する基本要素

（『現代高等英文法』pp. 2 〜 15, pp. 167 〜 181 に該当）

## 1 文とは

文は，動詞を中心にいくつかの語から成り立っています．その動詞は必ず主語をとり，目的語や補語を取ることがあります．このような複数の要素が順序よく並び，的確に意味を伝える文となっています．また文は，主部（主語を含む名詞句）と述部（述語動詞，補語，目的語）にわけられ，その述部の性質によって分類されたものを文型（sentence pattern）と言います．

I had a hard time falling asleep last night.

主部　　　述部　　（昨晩，寝つきが悪かった）

## 2 文型

文を構成する要素によって，英語の文は5つのパタンにわけられます．これらを5文型（five sentence patterns）と呼びます．Table 1.1.1 は，各文型とそれらを構成する要素，例文を記しています．

Table 1.1.1　5 文型

| 文型の名称 | 構成要素 | 例文 |
|---|---|---|
| 第 I 文型 | 主語（S）+ 動詞（V）+（副詞的語句（A）) | We walked and walked.<br>She went to Tokyo. |
| 第 II 文型 | 主語（S）+ 動詞（V）+ 補語（C） | John is difficult. |
| 第 III 文型 | 主語（S）+ 動詞（V）+ 目的語（O）+（副詞的語句（A）) | We like French.<br>She put the vase on the floor. |
| 第 IV 文型 | 主語（S）+ 動詞（V）+ 目的語（O）+ 目的語（O） | Mary made him coffee. |
| 第 V 文型 | 主語（S）+ 動詞（V）+ 目的語（O）+ 補語（C） | We call her Maria. |

構成要素の略は，次の通りです．S = subject（主語），V = predicative verb（述語動詞），C = complement（補語），O = object（目的語），A = adverbial（副詞的語句）．

### ！注意！

(1) 第 I 文型と第 III 文型の「（副詞的語句（A））」は，この要素が文中に現れる場合とそうでない場合があることを示しています．(2) 第 IV 文型には，目的語が 2 つありますが，1 つ目の目的語は間接目的語（indirect object），2 つ目の目的語は直接目的語（direct object）と言います．

　5 文型は，欧米の文法学者のさまざまな試行錯誤の結果，19 世紀末に完成しました．文型は，それらを構成している主語，述語動詞，補語，目的語の機能から分類したものです．副詞的語句が必要かどうかは，個々の動詞の特性であり，文型には直接関係がありません．

### <もっと詳しく>　☞『現代高等英文法』pp. 5ff.

「5 文型以外の文型の考え方」，「5 文型の歴史」

# 3 文を構成する基本要素

文を構成する基本要素の説明の前に，機能から見た語のグループである品詞 (parts of speech) について紹介します．本書が採用する品詞は，次の 10 品詞です．名詞 (noun, 略号 N)，代名詞 (pronoun, 略号 Pron.)，冠詞 (article, 略号 ART)，動詞 (verb, 略号 V)，助動詞 (auxiliary verb, 略号 AUX)，形容詞 (adjective, 略号 Adj.)，副詞 (adverb, 略号 Adv.)，前置詞 (preposition, 略号 Prep.)，接続詞 (conjunction, 略号 Conj.)，間投詞 (interjection, 略号 Inter.)．

## 3.1 主語

主語になるのは，(1) のイタリックが示すように主に名詞（句），to 不定詞，動名詞，節です．

- (1) a. *Those shoes* are not my size. [名詞句]
  - b. *To be absurd* is to be in violation of common sense. [to 不定詞]
  - c. *Doing nothing a whole day* is simply a bore. [動名詞]
  - d. *That he is lying* is apparent. (＝It is apparent that he is lying.) [節]

しかし，*Just because you are right* does not mean that I am wrong. のように，理由を表す副詞節 because が主語となる場合があります．この場合，Just because 〜 doesn't mean …（〜だからと言って，…ということにはならない）というフレーズとして使用される傾向にあります．ただし，このようなフレーズは改まった文章では避けられます．

### ＜もっと詳しく＞ ☞『現代高等英文法』pp. 9 〜 10
「主語は名詞句でなければならないか」

## 3.2　述語動詞

　述語動詞とは，文の中心をなす動詞（主動詞とも言います）だけでなく，時制，相，態，助動詞を含んだものを指します．(2) の例で，イタリックの箇所が述語動詞です．

- (2) a. The concert *is to be* over soon.
    - b. *Would* you *mind* if I smoke [or if I smoked]?
    - c. He *may be said* to be an excellent artist.
    - d. They *were singing* in a loud voice.
    - e. I*'ve had* enough, thank you.

(2) の例で見るように，述語動詞は「時制（助動詞）（相）（態）主動詞」から成り立ちます．（　）は任意の要素ですが，時制と主動詞は必須要素です．時制，助動詞，相，態，主動詞については，PART II で詳しく説明します．上記の「時制（助動詞）（相）（態）主動詞」で表すと，(2) の述語動詞の構成は (3) のようになります．

- (3) a. [現在]時制 [be to]助動詞 [be]主動詞
    - b. [過去]時制 [will]助動詞 [mind]主動詞
    - c. [現在]時制 [may]助動詞 [be＋過去分詞]態 [say]主動詞
    - d. [過去]時制 [be＋現在分詞]相 [sing]主動詞
    - e. [現在]時制 [have＋過去分詞]相 [have]主動詞

(3) で述語動詞の要素である「主動詞」は，品詞としては「動詞」で，「動詞」は目的語を取らない自動詞（intransitive verb）と目的語を取る他動詞（transitive verb）に分類されます．それらをさらに詳しく見ると，Table 1.1.2 のようになります．

Table 1.1.2　動詞の分類

| 動詞 | 自動詞<br>（目的語を<br>取らない） | 完全自動詞：目的語も補語も取らない<br>　　　　　　第 I 文型の動詞．A が必要な時もある |
|---|---|---|
| | | 不完全自動詞：補語を取る．第 II 文型の動詞 |
| | 他動詞<br>（目的語を<br>取る） | 完全他動詞：目的語を 1 つ取るが補語を取らない<br>　　　　　　第 III 文型の動詞．A が必要な時もある |
| | | 完全他動詞：目的語を 2 つ取るが補語を取らない<br>　　　　　　第 IV 文型の動詞 |
| | | 不完全他動詞：目的語と補語を取る動詞<br>　　　　　　第 V 文型の動詞 |

## ＜もっと詳しく＞　☞『現代高等英文法』p. 12

「法の扱い，無標と有標」

## 3.3　目的語

　目的語とは，動詞から何らかの働きかけを受ける名詞（句）およびそれに相当する語句・節のことです．動詞によって，どのようなタイプの目的語をとるかは決まっています（PART II 第 1 章 3）．(4) の例を見てください．イタリックの箇所が目的語です．(4d, e) で使用されている make, give は，目的語を 2 つとる場合（第 IV 文型）と目的語を 1 つとる場合（第 III 文型）があります．

(4) a.　I like *dogs*.

　　b.　John and Mary like *to travel abroad*.

　　c.　Do you believe *she will succeed*?

　　d.　They made *me a good cup of coffee*.

　　　　→ They made *a good cup of coffee* for me.

　　e.　Her parents *gave her a nice present*.

　　　　→ Her parents gave *a nice present* to her.

## 3.4　補語

(5) の例を見てください．補語は，(5a, b) の主格補語と (5c, d) の目的格補語に分けられます．主格補語は主語の状態などを説明するもので，目的格補語は目的語の状態などを説明するものです．

(5) a. The meat has gone *bad*.

b. It's *nice* sitting here with you.

c. Can't you smell something *burning*?

d. He likes his coffee *strong*.

## 3.5　その他の要素 ── 副詞的語句・独立語句・修飾要素

文は，上で述べた基本要素だけから成り立つことはまれです．基本要素以外に，副詞的語句，修飾要素，独立語句があります．これらは，文型を決めるための基本要素ではありませんが，動詞や文の意味を決定するために必要となることがあります．(6) の例を見てください．

(6) a. My wife lives **in Chicago**.

b. My office is **in the next building**.

c. Put the vase **on the table**.

d. Do you think it will snow **tonight**?

e. **When** are you leaving Japan?

f. We like French **better than English**.

g. We **usually** call her Maria.

h. Mary made him **a good cup of** coffee.

(6a, b, c) の場合，太字で示す副詞的語句が省略されると文法的に正しい文とはなりません．(6d, e) の場合，太字の副詞的語句がなくても文法的には問題ありませんが，正しく意味を伝えるためには必要な要素です．(6f, g, h) の太字の要素は，修飾要素です．

## 4   態 —— 第 III, IV, V 文型

態（voice）とは，主語と動詞の関係のあり方のことです．態は，能動態と受動態に分けられます．(7) の例を見てください．

(7) a.   They speak French.

（主語（they）と動詞（speak）は動作主と動作の関係
→ 能動態（active voice）の文）

   b.   French is spoken by them.

（主語（French）と動詞（speak）は動作を受ける対象と動作の関係
→ 受動態（passive voice）の文）

(7) からわかるように，受動態は「主語（能動態の目的語）＋ be 動詞＋動詞の過去分詞＋（by 能動態の主語の目的格）」という文法形式で表示されます．これまでに触れた第 III, IV, V 文型の文には目的語（名詞あるいは that 節に限ります）があるので，原則的に受動文に書き換えることができます．また第 IV 文型は目的語が 2 つあるので，2 種類の受動文ができます．但し，間接目的語である人を主語にした受動文が一般的です．(8), (9), (10) は，それぞれ第 III, IV, V 文型の能動文と受動文です（各例の a が能動文，b, c が受動文です）．

(8) a.   Mary *loves* her pet cat Michael.

   b.   Michael, Mary's pet cat, *is loved* by her.

(9) a.   My father *gave* me a present.

   b.   I *was given* a present.                    [間接目的語が主語に]

   c.   A present *was given* (to) me.              [直接目的語が主語に]

(10) a.   We *believe him to be* the finest violinist in the world.

   b.   He *is believed to be* the finest violinist in the world.

態を入れ替えると，通常は意味は変わります．しかし，(8a) と (8b) を比較するとわかるように，能動文と受動文は，機械的に転換できるわけではありません．(10) については，主語の目的語に対する信念を表す動詞，believe が使用さ

れています．believe のような動詞は，that 節をとる第 III 文型と書き換え可能
です（(10a) の場合，We believe that he is the finest violinist in the world. と
なります）．believe の場合，that 節 → to be (10a) と書き換えが可能です．
(10b) は，その (10a) の目的語である him を主語にした受動文です．

## 4.1　get 受動態 (*get*-passive)

　受動態は「主語（能動態の目的語）＋ be 動詞＋動詞の過去分詞」という文法形
式が基本ですが，「get ＋動詞の過去分詞」の文法形式で表示される get 受動態が
あります．以下の例を見てください．

(11) a.　A headmaster *got stabbed* a few weeks ago.　What is the world
　　　　　coming to?
　　b.　Liam *got promoted* again.　He's now the sales and marketing di-
　　　　　rector.

get 受動態は，動的な意味を持ちます．また，くだけた会話で使用され，意外な
ことを述べる際に使用されます．日本語では，基本的な受動態と get 受動態を区
別することは困難です．
　(11) の例では，get 受動態には動作主が表記されていませんが，(12) に示す
ように必要に応じて動作主を表すことができます．

(12) a.　I almost *got hit by* a bus.
　　b.　I don't *get paid by* the league.
　　c.　Did you *get attacked by* a seagull?

## ＜もっと詳しく＞　☞『現代高等英文法』p. 169
「got itself jammed は get 受動文か？」

## 4.2  受動態にできない他動詞

　すべての他動詞が，受動態にできるわけではありませんので，注意をしてください．受動態で使用されない例は，(13) の通りです．

(13) a.　They have a nice house. → ×A nice house is had by them.

　　 b.　They want to join the group. → ×To join the group is wanted.

　　 c.　He built the children a tree house.

　　　　 → ×The children were built a tree house.

　　 d.　The repair cost me a lot.

　　　　 → ×I was cost a lot by the repair.

　　 e.　Everybody wanted Doris to be the manager.

　　　　 → ×Doris was wanted to be the manager.

　　 f.　We like our staff to say what they think.

　　　　 → ×Our staff are liked to say what they think.

　　 g.　We couldn't make her understand us.

　　　　 → ×She couldn't be made to understand us.

(13a) に示す have は受動態にできません．(13b) の to 不定詞が目的語の場合は，動詞に関係なく受動態にできません．(13c, d) は第 IV 文型ですが，そのような動詞でも，直接に動作が及ばない間接目的語を主語にした受動態は使用されません．(13e, f) のように，願望の want や (would) like to は受動態にはできません．(13g) の make は強制的に「人に行為をさせる」ことができないため，受動態は不可となります．

## 4.3  注意すべき受動態

　(14) に示す動詞類は，受動態にできます．

(14) a.　This form must *be filled out* correctly and sent to the following e-mail address.

　　　　　　　　　　　　　　　　　　　　　　　　　　　　[句動詞]

b. The plan *has been looked at* carefully. ［前置詞動詞］

c. … he will be clearly recognized as someone to *be put up with* until his retirement age is reached. ［句前置詞動詞］

d. His argument should not *be made light of.* ［イディオム動詞］

受動態で by 以外の前置詞が使用される例を，(15) にあげます．

(15) a. I *was surprised at* what he said.

b. Chomsky *is known to* every linguist.

c. The floor *was covered with* plastic sheeting.

d. We *were* all *shocked at* the news of his death.

(15) で使用されている過去分詞は，形容詞扱いされることが一般的です．by は動作主を表すので，(15) で使用されている at, to, with などが使用される場合は違った意味となります．

## 4.4 受動態のほうが普通に使われる場合

英語では能動態が一般的に使用されるため，受動態を使用する際は理由があります．(16) の例を見てください．

(16) a. His father *was killed* in the war.

b. You *are* kindly *requested* to fasten your seatbelt.

c. This paper *was* originally *written* in 1993 but never appeared in print.

d. The Queen *has been photographed* riding in the grounds of Windsor.

(16a) は，動作主が不特定のため受動態の使用が典型的となります．(16b) は機内アナウンスで，誰が依頼しているかは重要ではありません．(16c) は論文などの堅い文章で，著者の I を避けて受動態が使用されています．近年の傾向として，最近の論文では受動態ではなく I が主語となった能動態の文章が問題なく

使用されます. (16d) は写真のキャプションで,誰が写真を撮ったかは問題と
なりません.


## 4.5 能動受動動詞

　英語の動詞には,形は能動文でありながら,意味的に受動文となるものがあり
ます. これは受動態として扱いますが,このような文を作る動詞は「能動受動動
詞」(activo-passive verb) もしくは「中間態動詞」(middle-voice verb),または
「中間動詞」(middle verb) とも呼ばれます. そして,このような動詞が使用さ
れた文は,能動受動文と言います. 下記の例を見てください.

 (17) a. This book *sells very well.*

   b. The novel *reads interesting.*

   c. Her voice *carries well.*

   d. This pen *writes smoothly.*


# ◉練習問題◉

## 1　5文型を使用した英文を作成しなさい.

第 I 文型：_____

第 II 文型：_____

第 III 文型：_____

第 IV 文型：_____

第 V 文型：_____


## 2　p. 7 にある (6) の英文 a～h の文型を書きなさい.

 (6) a. My wife lives in Chicago.

   b. My office is in the next building.

   c. Put the vase on the table.

    d.  Do you think it will snow tonight?

    e.  When are you leaving Japan?

    f.  We like French better than English.

    g.  We usually call her Maria.

    h.  Mary made him a good cup of coffee.

**3**  Oral translation: 以下の日本文を，指定された文型と単語もしくはフレーズを活用して英語で言いなさい．

3.1  このバスはダウンタウンに行きますか？　[I]

___

3.2  1 年は 12 ヶ月です．　[I, III]

[I]
___
[III]
___

3.3  このコーヒーはよい香りがする．　[II], smell good

___

3.4  山本先生は，英文学の専門家です．　[II], a specialist

___

3.5  彼女は私を双子の妹と間違えた．　[III], mistake A for B

___

3.6  あなたは彼が正直だと思いますか？　[III, V]

[III]
___
[V]
___

3.7  キリンを英語で何と言いますか？　[III], How / What do you …?

___

3.8  四つ葉のクローバーを見つけたことがありますか？　[III], a four-leaf clover

___

3.9  そのビルの高さを教えてくれますか？　[IV], Could you tell me …?

___

3.10 もう彼女に借金を払いましたか？　[IV], Have you …?, debt

___

3.11　彼の髪型は彼を若く見せる．　[V]

_____

3.12　彼の髪の毛は，いつもボサボサだ．　[V], leave, unkempt

_____

3.13　明日の朝は，雨が降るだろう．　[I, II, III]

　　　[I] _____

　　　[II] _____

　　　[III] _____

3.14　日本の大学は入るのは難しいが，出るのはやさしいと言われている．　[I, III]

　　　[I] _____

　　　[III] _____

3.15　その山の上の湖には，龍が棲むと言われている．　[I, III]

　　　[I] _____

　　　[III] _____


## 4　文の意味をよく考えて，（ ）内の動詞を [ ] 内の指示に従って正しい態に変えなさい．

4.1　This picture (always admire).　[現在]

_____

4.2　His leg (hurt) in an accident.　[過去]

_____

4.3　The answers must (write) on this side of the paper only.　[原形不定詞]

_____

4.4　Your question (answer)?　[現在完了]

_____

4.5　Entering the (crowd) room, the woman could not see even one person whom she knew.　[分詞]

_____

## 5 態を変えなさい.

5.1 Has someone fixed the chair yet?

_____

5.2 They invited me to their wedding reception.

_____

5.3 We saw him enter the store with his wife.

_____

5.4 All the biscuits were eaten up yesterday.

_____

5.5 Several assembly members are said to be involved in the bribery case.

_____

# 第2章 修飾要素，独立要素，文の種類

（『現代高等英文法』pp. 16 〜 42 に該当）

前章は，動詞を中心に文を構成する基本要素を説明しました．本章は，文で使用される修飾要素と独立要素を説明します．その後，そのような要素を活用した文の種類を説明します．

## 1 修飾語句

修飾語句（modifier）は，Table 1.2.1 にあるように形容詞的修飾語句（adjectival modifier）と副詞的修飾語句（adverbial modifier）があります．

Table 1.2.1 2種類の修飾語句

| 種類 | 修飾するもの | 働き | 例文 |
|---|---|---|---|
| 形容詞的修飾語句 | 名詞（句）を修飾 | 形容詞，形容詞句，形容詞節 | (1) |
| 副詞的修飾語句 | 名詞句，形容詞（句），副詞（句），動詞句，文を修飾 | 副詞，副詞句，副詞節 | (2) |

各例のイタリック体で表記している部分が修飾語句で，太字が修飾される語句（被修飾語と言います）です．

(1) a. He has a *high-bridged* **nose**.

b. **Students** *in this class* are all cheerful and spirited.

16

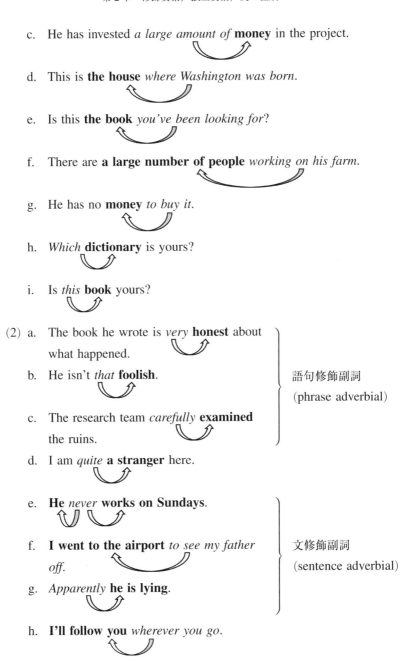

c. He has invested *a large amount of* **money** in the project.

d. This is **the house** *where Washington was born.*

e. Is this **the book** *you've been looking for*?

f. There are **a large number of people** *working on his farm.*

g. He has no **money** *to buy it.*

h. *Which* **dictionary** is yours?

i. Is *this* **book** yours?

(2) a. The book he wrote is *very* **honest** about what happened.

b. He isn't *that* **foolish**.

c. The research team *carefully* **examined** the ruins.

d. I am *quite* **a stranger** here.

語句修飾副詞 (phrase adverbial)

e. **He** *never* **works on Sundays**.

f. **I went to the airport** *to see my father off*.

g. *Apparently* **he is lying**.

文修飾副詞 (sentence adverbial)

h. **I'll follow you** *wherever you go*.

## 2　独立要素

　独立要素には，(3) に示す間投詞 (ah, oh, oops, hello など)，(4) に示す副詞 (yes, yeah, no など)，(5) に示す他動詞から変化した副詞 (please)，(6) に示す談話辞 (you bet, you know などの文が変化したもの) があります.

(3) a.　*Ah*, he is coming!（彼が来ることは予測通り）

    b.　*Oh*, he is coming!（彼が来ることは予測していない）

    c.　You are Japanese, *huh / eh*?

      （前者はアメリカ用法，後者はカナダ用法）

    d.　*Hi*, Jane, how are you?

間投詞は文脈に応じてさまざまな意味を持つことがわかってきたので，近年の学習者用英和辞典では詳しく説明しています.

(4)　Haven't you been in the States for a long time?

    —*No*, I've been in Canada.

    —*Yes*, I've been there for three years.

(4) の yes, no は副詞の一種です.

(5) a.　Would you *please* come with me?

    b.　Two coffees, *please*.

    c.　"We have lots more coffee. Would you like another cup?"—"Yes, *please*"

    d.　Oh, *please*. That's enough.

　please を使用すれば丁寧な言い方になると聞いたことがあるかもしれませんが，実態はそうではありません. (5a) の Would you please come with me? は Will you please come with me? よりも丁寧な言い方ですが，人に依頼をする場合に使用するよりよい丁寧表現があります. それは，Could you possibly ～? です.

**＜もっと詳しく＞**　☞『**現代高等英文法**』p. 20

「please の語源」

(6) a.　We are not talking about such a thing, *you see*.

　　b.　*You know*, most of the time he seems like such a fool.

　　c.　*You know what*?—What?—I'm getting hungry.

間投詞と同じく，(6) の談話辞も文脈に応じて意味が異なるため，研究が活発に行われ，その研究成果の一部が辞典の記述に反映されています．

# 3　節と句

　文の種類を説明する前に，文を構成する単位である節（clause）と句（phrase）について説明します．

## 3.1　節

　節は，「主部＋時制を持った述部」から成り立ちます．(7) の例を見てください．それぞれの例の節を [　　] で示しています．

(7) a.　[How are you doing]?

　　b.　[I don't like the way] [he talks].

　　c.　[Although she has been working for the company for only seven months], [she says] [that she is always looking for other opportunities].

　　d.　[He switched off the television] and [went to bed].

(7b, c, d) は，複数の節から成り立っています．そのような場合，(7b) の I don't like the way は文の中心になっているので，主節（main clause）と言い，he talks は主節の意味を補うので従属節（subordinate clause）と言います．それ

では，(7c) の主節と従属節はどれでしょうか．she says が主節で，Although she has been ～ seven months と that she is ～ opportunities が従属節です．(7d) の場合は，どうでしょうか．(7d) は He switched off the television と went to bed という主節 2 つが等位接続詞（PART III 第 4 章）(and や or など) で結びつけられています．このように，等位接続詞で接続された節を等位節といいます．

　等位接続詞以外に，接合詞（接続副詞ともいいます）が (8) に示すように，文を結合する場合もあります（詳しくは PART III 第 4 章を参照してください）．

(8)　We must hurry; *otherwise* we'll miss the train.

## 3.2　句

　句は，主部と述部を持たないかたまりで，まとまった意味を持ち，いろいろな文法的機能（名詞句，形容詞句，副詞句，動詞句）を果たします．(9) で使用されている句を（　　）で示し，文法機能を明記します．

(9) a.　(His family) (lived) (happily) (in (a little apartment)) (in (Tokyo)).
　　　　名詞句　　　　動詞句　副詞句　　（副詞句 (名詞句)）　　（副詞句 (名詞句)）
　　 b.　(I) (have (an American friend)) (working for (a computer company)).
　　　　名詞句　（動詞句 (名詞句)）　　　（形容詞句 (名詞句)）

## 4　文の種類

　文は，その形態から分類される場合と，その意味から分類される場合にわけられます．

## 4.1　形態からの分類

　形態から文を分類すると，単文 (simple sentence)，複文 (complex sen-

tence），重文（compound sentence），重複文（compound-complex sentence）が
あります．

(10) a. [He wants to know the best way to lose weight.]

　　　　　　　　　　　　　　　　　　　　[単文：1つの節からなる]

　　 b. [I learned some alphabet signs] [when I was in America.]

　　　　　　　　[複文：主節と1つまたはそれ以上の従属節からなる]

　　 c. [Left-handedness is becoming more acceptable in society], [and is
even considered advantageous in some sports].

　　　　　　[重文：等位接続詞で結合される2つ以上の等位節からなる]

　　 d. [Designing may seem simple], but [only those [who are creative,
practical and sensitive to people's needs] can be successful de-
signers].

[重複文：主節と従属節からなるが，主節あるいは従属節，もしくは両方の
節が等位節からなる文]

## 4.2　意味からの分類

　意味に基づくと，文は平叙文（declarative sentence），疑問文（question/inter-
rogative sentence），感嘆文（exclamatory sentence），命令文（imperative sen-
tence）にわけられます．それぞれの文に，肯定文（affirmative sentence）と否定
文（negative sentence）があります．Table 1.2.2 を見てください．

Table 1.2.2　意味に基づく文の分類

| 文の種類 | 下位分類 | 例文 |
|---|---|---|
| 平叙文 | 該当なし | (11) |
| 疑問文 | wh 疑問文 (*wh*-question) | (13) |
| | yes-no 疑問文 (*yes-no* question)<br>一般疑問文 (general question) | (14) |
| | 付加疑問文 (tag-question) | (15), (17), (18) |
| | エコー疑問文 (echo-question) | (19) |
| | 間接疑問文 (indirect question) | (20) |
| | 文末疑問詞疑問文<br>(sentence-final *wh*-word interrogative) | (22) |
| 感嘆文 | what 感嘆文 (*what*-exclamatory sentence) | (23), (24) |
| | how 感嘆文 (*how*-exclamatory sentence) | (23), (24) |
| | 間接感嘆文 (indirect exclamatory sentence) | (25) |
| 命令文 | 通常の命令文，命令文 + or / and … | (26) |
| | let 命令文 (*let*-imperative) | (27), (28) |

## 4.2.1　平叙文

平叙文は，事実をそのまま述べる文です．

(11) a.　You should take care not to catch cold.

     b.　I'll come to your office at five p.m.

## 4.2.2　疑問文

疑問文は，聞き手に疑問を問う文です．Table 1.2.2 にあるように，6 つの種類があります．

**4.2.2.1**　wh 疑問文

wh 疑問文は，wh 疑問詞（wh-question）である who, which, when, where, why, how のいずれかを使った疑問文です．この疑問詞のうち，who, which は疑問代名詞（interrogative pronoun），when, where, how, why は疑問副詞（interrogative adverb）といいます．疑問副詞は，それぞれ「時」，「場所」，「方法」，「理由」を聞きます（詳しくは，PART III 第 6 章を見てください）．

wh 疑問文の基本的文法形式は，次のとおりです．

(12)　a.　一般動詞の場合：「wh 疑問詞＋助動詞（do, does, did, have, has）＋主語＋動詞の原形（do, does, did の場合）／動詞の過去分詞（have, has の場合）〜？」

　　　b.　be 動詞の場合：「wh 疑問詞＋be 動詞（am, are, is, was, were）＋主語＋〜？」

(13)　a.　*How* do you come to school?—I come to school by bus and train./I walk to school.

　　　b.　*When* did you get married?

　　　c.　*Why* did she run away?

　　　d.　*Who* do you believe is the best player on the team?

　　　e.　*Which* time suits you better—12:30 or one o'clock?

(13d) は，do you believe が挿入句として使用されている wh 疑問文です．(13e) は，wh 疑問詞を使用して 12 時 30 分か 1 時のどちらかを選択するため，「選択疑問文」といいます．

**4.2.2.2**　yes-no 疑問文

yes, no で答え，疑問詞を使用しない疑問文を，yes-no 疑問文もしくは一般疑問文といいます．この疑問文の作り方は，①操作詞を文頭に置く，②主語をその後に置く，です．

(14)　a.　Are you from Africa?—No, I'm from the U.S.

　　　b.　Can't you believe me?—Yes, of course I can.

但し，上記に述べた作り方ではなく，（14a）を平叙文にした You are from Africa. の文末を上昇調（↗）で発音した場合，yes-no 疑問文となります．このような上昇調の平叙疑問文は，会話で使用される傾向にあります．

### 4.2.2.3  付加疑問文

付加疑問文は，平叙文の末尾に確認や同意を求めるために，疑問を表す節を付加したものです．注意点は，主節である文が肯定か否定かで付加する節の形式が異なります．また，命令文（肯定の場合）の付加節は shall we? もしくは will you? となります．（15）を見てください．

(15) a.  Her mother is now over ninety years old, *isn't she*?
     b.  You haven't had your hair cut for a month, *have you*?
     c.  Let's have a potluck party tomorrow, *shall we*?
     d.  Stand up, *will you*?

付加疑問文の形は，（16）に示すとおりです．

(16) a.  肯定文 , 操作詞の否定形＋主語を代名詞にしたもの  ＝（15a）
     b.  否定文 , 操作詞の肯定形＋主語を代名詞にしたもの  ＝（15b）

付加節が上昇調（↗）の場合は聞き手に確認をし，下降調（↘）の場合は聞き手に同意を求めます．

（16）で述べたように，付加疑問文を作るには主語を代名詞に変える必要があります．nobody, everybody 等が使用された文の付加疑問文は，（17）のようになります．

(17) a.  Nobody came, did *they*?
     b.  Everybody was happy, weren't *they*?
     c.  Nothing happened, did *it*?
     d.  Everything was all right, wasn't *it*?

(17a, b) のように，nobody, everybody の付加疑問節は単数ですが，複数形の操作詞及び性差を問わない they を使います．一方，（17c, d）のように物を表す

nothing, everything の付加疑問文は，単数の it を使用します.

　I am .... の付加疑問文は，(18) に示すように aren't I となります.

　(18)　I'm allowed to have oysters, *aren't I*?

## ＜もっと詳しく＞　☞『**現代高等英文法**』p. 28f.

「(1) am の否定形」，「(2) 反復付加文」

### 4.2.2.4　エコー疑問文

　エコー疑問文は，会話で使用され，相手の発言の聞き取れなかった部分や確認したい部分を，疑問詞に替えたものです. (19) の例を見てください.

　(19) a.　John's family is originally from Ukraine.—His family is from *where* (↗)?

　　　b.　My desk is made of mahogany.—Your desk is made of *what* (↗)?

　　　c.　She'll finish the work by the end of the month.—By *when* (↗)?

(19a) の場合，名詞の Ukraine を疑問副詞である where で聞いているのは，場所であることがわかっているからです. (19b) は mahogany という物が聞き取れなかったため，それを what で聞いています. (19c) は名詞句 the end of month を疑問副詞の when で聞いています.

### 4.2.2.5　間接疑問文

　間接疑問文は，疑問文が文の一部になっているものです. (20) のイタリック体の箇所が，間接疑問文です.

　(20) a.　I'm interested to know *how cheese is made from milk*.

　　　b.　Do you know *who invented the telephone*?

　　　c.　Do you happen to know *if he speaks Japanese*?

　　　d.　Could you tell me *where we are*?

　　　e.　I'm guessing *what's going to happen next*.

　　　f.　Nobody wants to decide *whether the president had committed a crime.*

g.　*How the story ends* is still unknown.

h.　The question is *whether or not he really knew it.*

i.　I'm interested in *how we can improve the situation.*

j.　We don't care (about) *who you were before you got here.*

(20a, b, c, d, e, f) の間接疑問文は動詞の目的語，(20g) は主語，(20h) は be 動詞の補語，(20i, j) は前置詞の目的語になっています．(20g) の間接疑問文が主語の場合，主語が長くなるので，仮主語として代理の it を使用し，間接疑問文を末尾に移動させる傾向にあります (It is still unknown *how the story ends.*)．(20j) で (about) となっている理由は，意味解釈上問題がない場合は前置詞が省略されることがあるためです．多くの場合，間接疑問文は平叙文と同じ語順になります．

　(20a, b, d, e) の wh 疑問が間接疑問の場合，疑問詞は先頭の位置のままで変更はありません．では，どのように wh 疑問文が間接疑問文になるのか (20a, b) を例に説明します．(21) を見てください．

(21) a.　How is cheese made from milk?

　　　　→ I'm interested to know how cheese is made from milk.

　　b.　Who invented the telephone?

　　　　→ Do you know who invented the telephone?

(21a) は is と cheese の語順が入れ替わり，平叙文と同じ語順になります．(21b) の場合は who が主語であるため語順に変化なく，平叙文と同じ語順です．

　(20d, e) が示すように，間接疑問文を導く動詞として tell, guess があります．動詞以外に，We still can't *be certain* who is going to win. のように形容詞 (be certain) も間接疑問文を導きます．これ以外の動詞・形容詞として，agree, argue, ask, be certain, be careful, be concerned, be sure, check, confirm, decide, doubt, estimate, explain, find out, know, learn, prove, show, wonder などがあります．詳しくは『現代高等英文法』(p. 31) を参照してください．

　(20c) は if が使用されていますが，これは yes-no 疑問文が間接疑問になった

例です．whether を使用しても問題ありませんが，堅苦しい印象を与えます．(20c) の場合，Do you happen to know? + does he speak Japanese? から成り立っています．(20f) の Nobody wants to decide whether the president had committed a crime. は，Nobody wants to decide + had the president committed a crime? から成り立っています．

## ＜もっと詳しく＞　☞『現代高等英文法』p. 31ff.

「whether と if」，「(1) wh 疑問文と間接疑問文」，「(2) wh 節の主節化と主節の挿入節化」，「(3) (2) の動詞のリスト」

### 4.2.2.6　文末疑問詞疑問文

　文末疑問詞疑問文は，通常の wh 疑問文を作成するための操作である①訊ねたい部分を疑問詞に置き換える，②疑問詞を文頭に出す，③疑問文の語順にする，のうち①のみで作られるものです．エコー疑問文と同じように，スピード感のあるきびきびとした会話で使用されます．しかし，エコー疑問文と異なり，聞き取れなかったことを wh 疑問詞で聞き返すのではなく，これまでの会話を発展させ，新しい情報を得るために使用されます．(22) の例を見てください．

(22)　a.　So you boarded the train *where*?—At Los Angeles.

　　　b.　He's the son of Governor Jeb Bush.  Your father arrived *when*?

### 4.2.3　感嘆文

　感嘆文は驚きを表し，what 感嘆文と how 感嘆文があります．(23) の例を見てください．

(23)　a.　It is a nice day today. → What a nice day (it is) today!
　　　　　　　　　　　　　　　　　副詞　名詞句

　　　b.　It is clear today. → How clear it is today!
　　　　　　　　　　　　　　副詞 形容詞

　　　c.　*What/How fun* it is to ride and sing a sleighing song tonight!

(23a) の what 感嘆文は，名詞句 [a nice day] を副詞 what で強めています．そして，what a nice day を文頭に持ってきて what 感嘆文となっています．(23b) の how 感嘆文は，形容詞 clear を how が強めて，how clear を文頭に持ってきて how 感嘆文となっています．(23c) の場合，what/how の後に fun が使用されています．この fun（楽しみ）は名詞ですので，本来は what 感嘆文で使用されます．しかし fun は他の名詞と異なり，冠詞を取らないので形容詞と解釈され，how 感嘆文となることもあります．

　次に，what 感嘆文と how 感嘆文の違いを説明します．下記の例を見てください．

   (24)  a.   *What [a difficult problem] we have on our hands!*

         b.   *What [difficult problems] we have on our hands!*

         c.   *What [difficult work] we have on our hands!*

         d.   *How difficult a problem we have on our hands!*

         e.   ×*How difficult problems we have on our hands!*

         f.   ×*How difficult work we have on our hands!*

what 感嘆文は，(24a, b, c) の例にあるように，[　] で示す単数，複数，不可算名詞の名詞句が使用可能です．how 感嘆文は，(24d) が示すように名詞句が単数で冠詞 a を伴う場合にのみ使用可能です．(24e, f) のように，名詞句が複数や不可算名詞の場合は使用できません．

### 4.2.3.1　間接感嘆文

　間接疑問文のように感嘆文が文の一部となり，間接感嘆文になる場合があります．その例を (25) に示します．

   (25)  a.  She was surprised at *what a nice person this Cameron seemed to be.*

         b.  I was surprised at *how many parents opposed this.*

         c.  She shuddered at the thought of *how close she was to destroying herself.*

(25) の what / how 間接感嘆文は，前置詞の目的語となっています．注意点は，①間接感嘆文の語順は元の感嘆文と同じ，②間接疑問文と異なり，間接感嘆文の前にある前置詞の省略はまれ，ということです（PART III 第 3 章に It is Adj. ＋間接感嘆文の記述があります）．

### 4.2.4　命令文

命令文は，動詞の原形を文頭に持ってきて，聞き手に指示・命令・勧誘・要求・嘆願などを表します．否定文は「Don't ＋ be / 動詞の原形〜．」という文法形式で表され，指示・命令・勧誘・要求・嘆願などを強調する場合は do が使用されます．下記の例を見てください．

(26) a. *Turn off* the TV and *listen to* me.
　　 b. *Don't run around* in the room.
　　 c. *Don't be* so noisy in the classroom.
　　 d. *Do sew* on the button right away.
　　 e. *Don't take* your eyes off my back **or** you'll get lost.
　　 f. *Knock* the door **and** it will be open to you.

(26e, f) の文法形式「命令文＋ or / and …」は，「〜しなさい，さもなければ / そうすれば…」という意味になります．

命令を伝える相手は，通常 you であるので you を文中で表す必要はありませんが，**You** be quiet! / **Everybody** go home! のように，you やそれ以外の相手を呼びかけ語で表す場合があります．

(26) の例以外に，料理手順（レシピ）でも動詞で始まる文が使用されます（例：*Heat* the oven（オーブンを温める）/ *Slice* the onion（玉ねぎを薄く切る））．これは，料理を作る人に命令をしているのではなく，You heat the oven. / You slice the onion. のように，heat, slice を行う行為者（つまり主語）が誰か明らかなので，その主語を省略した形となっています．

### 4.2.4.1　let 命令文

*Let's take a look at it.* のような命令文は let 命令文と言われ，聞き手に対し

ての指示を表します．この let's は let us の縮約形で，話し手と聞き手の両方を
含んでいます．Let us ... は，堅苦しくなります．Let's の否定文は，(27) に示
すように2種類ありますが，(27b) はイギリス用法です．

(27) a. Let's *not* take a look at it.
    b. *Don't* let's take a look at it.

let の目的語は，(28) に示すように物（= it）も可能です．

(28)   Don't *let* it worry you.

(27)，(28) 以外に動詞を省略して，副詞辞（PART III 第4章を参照してください）
のみの表現も可能で，主に話し言葉で使用されます．

(29) a. *Let* him **in**.
    b. *Let* it **out**.


#### 4.2.4.2  命令文以外の命令的な意味を持つ表現

　動詞の原形を文頭に使用する以外の命令の意味を持つ表現として，(30) の例
をあげます．

(30) a. You *will* be here by six tomorrow morning.
    b. You *had better* follow my advice.
    c. You *must* come and see me sometimes.
    d. You *are cordially requested* to take off your shoes before coming
       into this house.
    e. The doctor *advises* you take this medicine regularly after each
       meal.
    f. You *are to* be here by six tomorrow morning.
    g. *It is imperative that* the public be informed about these dangers.

(30a, b, c) は，きつい命令もしくは脅迫と取られかねないので，特別な場合以
外は避けたほうが賢明です．

# 5 否定

　平叙文，疑問文，命令文には，肯定文と否定文があります．肯定文は，否定語 (not, never, seldom, scarcely) を使用しないものです．否定文は，その否定語を使用するものです．(31) を見てください．

(31) a. *Don't* stay at the entrance.

b. She *didn't* want to buy anything at the supermarket.

c. She is *seldom* at home.

He comes back *only* on weekends. の only は「…しか…でない」という否定的な意味ですが，否定語ではありません．また，nobody, nothing を含む文（例：*Nobody* knows how they came to the conclusion.）は，nobody, nothing が否定の意味を持ちますが否定文を作るわけではありません．

## 5.1 部分否定

　部分否定の一般的な使用は，主語に every が含まれている場合や，副詞の always がある場合です．

(32) a. *Every* confession does *not* have 100 percent of the truth in it, because they don't give you the whole truth.

b. Computer science is *not always* seen as a priority.

次に，曖昧性を持つ以下の例を見てください．

(33) 　*All* the members of the committee have *not* signed the petition.

(33) のように，主語に all を含む文が否定形になると，(a) not が文全体を否定する文否定 (sentence negation) と (b) all を否定する語句否定 (phrase negation)，という 2 つの解釈が可能となります．(a) の場合は「委員会のメンバー全員が署名していませんでした」という意味になり，(b) の場合は「委員会のメン

バー全員が請願に署名したわけではありませんでした」という意味になります.
このような曖昧性を解消した文否定は, *None* of the members of the committee
have signed the petition. となります.

　似たような例として, both は全部否定もしくは部分否定か不明瞭になるので,
否定文での使用は避けられます (例: ?I do*n't* want *both* (of the) books. ◯ I
do*n't* want *either* of the books.)

## ◉練習問題◉

**1　単文, 複文, 重文, 重複文を自由に英作しなさい.**

単文: _____

複文: _____

重文: _____

重複文: _____

**2　間接疑問文, エコー疑問文, let 命令文, 間接感嘆文を自由に英作しなさい.**

間接疑問文: _____

エコー疑問文: _____

let 命令文: _____

間接感嘆文: _____

**3　Oral translation: (　　) 内の指示に従って, 訳しなさい.**

3.1　あの人に駅へ行く道をたずねてみよう.（単文と複文両方）

　　　（単文）_____

　　　（複文）_____

3.2　英語を読むのは得意ですが, 書くのは苦手です.（重文）

　　　_____

3.3　わからない単語が出てきたら, 辞書を引きなさい.（複文）

　　　_____

3.4　天気予報では晴れると言っていたが，雨になった．（重複文）

_____

3.5　今日の夜，メールしてください．

_____

3.6　明日から 3 日間会社が休みだ．

_____

3.7　A:「明日，お休みをいただきたいのですが？」
　　　B:「何をいただきたいって？」

_____

_____

3.8　A:「それでどこの駅で降りたって？」
　　　B:「サンディエゴです」

_____

_____

3.9　フェルトペンではなく，ボールペンで書いてください．

_____

3.10　私の言う通りにしなさい．さもないと，単位を取得できませんよ．

_____

## 4　（　　）の語句を使用して，日本語を英語に訳しなさい．

4.1　今から夏休みが待ち遠しい．(look forward to)

_____

4.2　明日は創立記念日で学校は休みだ．(the school foundation day)

_____

4.3　今日は，経済学の講義が休みだから図書館で勉強しよう．(cancel)

_____

4.4　今日はお客さんが少なかったから，のんびりできた．(be not so busy)

_____

4.5　今日はお客さんがたくさん見えるから，2 階へ行ってなさい．

_____

PART
II

# 述語動詞構成要素と準動詞

# 第1章　動詞と動詞型

（『現代高等英文法』pp. 44 〜 88 に該当）

## 1　動詞

### 1.1　動詞の活用変化

　動詞（verb）は文中で最も重要な働きをします．動詞は文型を決めるだけでなく，文で表現されている内容がいつのことか（時制），それが継続中か完了しているか（相），自ら能動的に行ったことか誰かから受けた行為か（態）といったことも表す役目を担います．これらを表すために動詞は，原形（root）という基本形に加えて，現在形（present），過去形（past），現在分詞形（present participle, 略号 ING(P)），過去分詞形（past participle, 略号 PP），動名詞形（gerund, 略号 ING(G)）という変化形を持ちます．例えば，look は，look（原形，三人称単数以外の現在形），looks（3 人称単数現在形），looked（過去形・過去分詞形），looking（現在分詞形，動名詞形）という変化をします．そして look — looks — looked — looking という変化を活用変化（conjugation）と言います．

### 1.2　規則変化と不規則変化

　動詞の活用変化には，規則変化（regular conjugation）と不規則変化（irregular conjugation）があります．過去形・過去分詞形を作るのに -ed または -d を用いるものは規則変化の動詞です．過去形・過去分詞形が wrote / written のように，原形 write から形と発音が変わってしまうものが不規則変化の動詞です．不規則変化する動詞には，go, come, eat, see, run など日常的によく使われるものが多

くあります．一方，現代英語において不規則変化・規則変化の両方を持つ動詞も
あります（例えば dive がその例です）．

## 1.3　動詞の変化表

be 動詞，have，look，write が，主語と時制に応じてどう変化するかを一覧表
にしたものが Table 2.1.1 です．

Table 2.1.1　主語の数と時制による動詞の変化表

| 動詞 | | be | | have | | look | | write | |
|---|---|---|---|---|---|---|---|---|---|
| 時制 | | 現在 | 過去 | 現在 | 過去 | 現在 | 過去 | 現在 | 過去 |
| 単数 | 1 人称 | am | was | have | had | look | looked | write | wrote |
| | 2 人称 | are | were | have | had | look | looked | write | wrote |
| | 3 人称 | is | was | has | had | looks | looked | writes | wrote |
| 複数 | 1 人称 | are | were | have | had | look | looked | write | wrote |
| | 2 人称 | are | were | have | had | look | looked | write | wrote |
| | 3 人称 | are | were | have | had | look | looked | write | wrote |

### ＜もっと詳しく＞　☞『現代高等英文法』p. 45
「go の過去形はなぜ went か」，「be 動詞はなぜ複雑な変化をするのか」

## 2　定形と非定形

（1）の 2 つの文には want（下線部）と be（イタリック）という 2 つの動詞が
含まれていますが，節の中心になる want は主語や時制によってどの変化形を使
うかが決まります．主語の人称・数，時制で決まる動詞の形を定形（finite）と言
います．「定形」というのは「決まっているひとつの形しかない」ということでは
なく，主語や時制によって「形が定まる」という意味です．一方，（1）の be は
時制もありませんし，主語の人称・数に影響を受けません．形が変わりませんの

で，非定形 (non-finite) と言います．主語や時制によって「形が定まらない」の
です．

    (1) a.　I <u>want</u> to *be* a teacher like my mother.

        b.　He <u>wants</u> to *be* a teacher like his mother.

        c.　I <u>wanted</u> to *be* a teacher like my mother.

(2) の例では下線部 want, likes, has が定形で，イタリック体 eat, skiing, gone
は非定形です．動詞の定形を持った節や文を定形節（文）(finite clause / sentence) と呼びます．非定形については PART II 第 6 章を見てください．

    (2) a.　I <u>want</u> to *eat* dinner early today.

        b.　She <u>likes</u> *skiing*.

        c.　He <u>has</u> *gone* somewhere.

# 3　5 文型と動詞型

## 3.1　自動詞と他動詞

  文型は，動詞によって決まります．目的語をとらない自動詞は第 I, II 文型に
現れ，目的語をとる他動詞は第 III, IV, V 文型に現れます．

  第 I 文型に現れる動詞は補語をとらない「完全自動詞」(complete intransitive
verb)，第 II 文型に現れる動詞は補語を必要とするので「不完全自動詞」(incomplete intransitive verb) と言います．第 III 文型に現れる他動詞は目的語を
とり，その後に補語を必要としませんので「完全他動詞」(complete transitive
verb)，第 V 文型に現れる動詞は目的語のあとに補語を必要としますので「不完
全他動詞」(incomplete transitive verb) と言います．また，第 IV 文型に現れる
目的語をふたつとる動詞を与格動詞 (dative verb) と呼びます．(8) の例のように，
ひとつの動詞が意味に応じていくつかの文型に現れるのは珍しくありません．

(3)　They *went* to Seattle to see a ball game　　　　[第 I 文型, 完全自動詞]

(4)　The perfume *smells* sweet.　　　　　　　　　[第 II 文型, 不完全自動詞]

(5)　What *causes* earthquakes?　　　　　　　　　[第 III 文型, 完全他動詞]

(6)　They *gave* her a lot of respect.　　　　　　　[第 IV 文型, 与格動詞]

(7)　*Call* me Mike.　　　　　　　　　　　　　[第 V 文型, 不完全他動詞]

(8)　a.　He *made* a good start.　　　　　　　　　　　[第 III 文型]

　　b.　He *made* us good coffee.　　　　　　　　　　[第 IV 文型]

　　c.　Does that *make* him a good person?　　　　　　[第 V 文型]

　自動詞＋前置詞全体がひとつの他動詞のような働きをする場合があります. これを前置詞動詞と呼びます.

(9)　They *arrived* at Tokyo.　　　　　　　　　　　　　[完全自動詞]

(10)　They *arrived at* the conclusion.　　　　　　　　　[自動詞＋前置詞]

　このふたつの文では同じ arrive at が使われていますが, (9) の「場所に到達する」の意味では, 前置詞が時に in や on になったりすることがあります. このようなものは arrive の自動詞が [at / in / on NP] の場所句を取っていると分析できます. この場所句は there に置き換えることができることからも arrive は自動詞とわかります. 一方で (10) の「結論に達する」の意味では arrive at が全体として他動詞のような働きをします. この場合は at をほかの前置詞に変えることができませんし, at the conclusion を there にすることもできません. また, This conclusion *was* finally *arrived at* after days of thorough discussion. のような受身になる可能性があります.

## 3.2　自動詞と他動詞の対応

　動詞によっては以下のような自動詞, 他動詞の対応関係を持ちます. それぞれの意味の違いにも注意しましょう.

　能格動詞 (ergative verb) は, 他動詞の目的語が自動詞の主語になるという対応関係を持つ動詞です. break, close などがあります (例：The door opened and a stranger came in./My girlfriend opened the door and came in.).

　働きかけ動詞（conative verb）と呼ばれる動詞があります．他動詞が at や on を取って自動詞になり，行為の影響をおよぼすことではなく，その行為をしようとする働きかけを表すものです．beat, hit, kick, knock, punch, shoot などがこの形を取ります．この自動詞＋at/on NP の形を「動能構文」と言うこともあります（例：He kicked at the sheet of paper to get it inside.（彼は部屋の中に入れようとして紙を何度も蹴る仕草をした））．

　She reads the newspaper every day. と She reads every day. は一見すると似ていますが，後者は「読書をする」という意味であって，何を読んでもいいということではありません．このように他動詞の目的語が省略されて自動詞になると，意味が特殊化することがあります．このような対応関係を持つものに，bake, cook, eat, fish, study, teach, write などがあります．

　古い英語では動詞＋oneself のような形であったものは，今では再帰代名詞 oneself を省略して使うのがふつうです．これらには wash, shave, dress, drown などがあります．

## ＜もっと詳しく＞　☞『現代高等英文法』p. 51
「「検査する」の意味を表す動詞 test の文型」

## 3.3　動詞型

　文型とは別に，動詞がどのような種類の補部（名詞句，形容詞句, that 節, (to) 不定詞，ING(G)，wh 節など）をとるのかという観点から分類したものを動詞型（verb pattern）と言います．動詞は意味に応じてどのような動詞形をとるのかが決まります．多様な動詞形をとる tell の意味を調べましょう．

(11)　Ben often *tells lies*.                          [第 III 文型，V＋N]

(12)　The teacher *told* us *about the plane crash*.

[第 III 文型，V＋N＋Prep.＋N]

(13)　The teacher often *tells us jokes*.              [第 IV 文型，V＋N＋N]

(14)　The professor *told me that I would flunk in math.*

[第 IV 文型，V＋N＋that 節]

(15)　She *told us how to solve the problem.*　　[第 IV 文型，V＋N＋wh 節]

(16)　He *told us to come to the front.*　　[第 V 文型，V＋N＋to 不定詞]

# 4　第 I 文型　S V (A)

　完全自動詞がとる文型では，場所や時などを表す副詞句を伴うことが多くあります．このような副詞句をここでは A と記号化します．例えば I walked, walked and walked. (私は歩きに歩いた) の文型は，S V ですが，We walked five miles. (5 マイル歩いた) のような文では S V A となります．

(17)　We *stopped* to have (a) rest.　　[完全自動詞＋副詞用法の to 不定詞]

(18)　A dog *came* running.　　[完全自動詞＋付帯状況の分詞構文]

(19)　My dad *is* in the kitchen preparing dinner.

[完全自動詞＋場所を表す副詞句]

(20)　It's *snowing* again.　　[完全自動詞，非人称動詞]

there 構文も，本書では第 I 文型と考えることにします．

(21)　*There were* many bribery cases in the last general election.

(22)　*There stands* a beautiful house near the lake.

there 構文では，疑問文では Are there …? のようになります．be 動詞の数を決めるのは be 動詞の後に来る名詞です．また (22) のように，be 動詞の代わりに seem, appear, happen, arrive, begin, come, exist, stand のような存在・出現・生起などを表す自動詞が使われることがあります．

### ＜もっと詳しく＞　☞『現代高等英文法』p. 55

「なぜ there 構文が必要なのか」，「Here's … という表現はどんな時に使われるか」

# 5　第 II 文型　S V C

## 5.1　連結動詞

　第 II 文型に使われる動詞を連結動詞 (copulative verb) と言い，以下のような
ものがあります．

Table 2.1.2　連結動詞の種類

| be 動詞 | is, am, are, was, were, been | A whale *is* a mammal. My dream has always *been* to have flying lessons. |
|---|---|---|
| 感覚動詞 | appear, feel, look, seem, smell, sound, taste など | This steak *tastes* funny. You *look* amazing. I love the new hairstyle. |
| 維持動詞（状態を維持する） | remain, keep, stay など | *Stay* calm. |
| 結果動詞（「…になる」） | become, come, end up, get, go, grow, prove など | The beer has *gone* stale. |

第 II 文型で使われる be 動詞には，主語を説明する用法 (She is happy. / A
whale is a mammal.) と，主語を同定する用法 (Mary is our teacher. / The City
Hall is the next stop.) があります．同定する用法では主語と補語を入れ替える
ことができます (Our teacher is Mary. / The next stop is the City Hall.)．
　完全自動詞が補語を取って連結動詞になることがあります（連結動詞化）．
(例：My father died young. / The spaghetti arrived steaming hot.)

## 5.2　補語

　補語になるのは形容詞や名詞（句，節）です．全体として形容詞に相当する前
置詞句も補語になります．(24) の in good health は healthy に相当します．こ

のようなフレーズには out of breath, out of order, of importance, of interest などがあります.

(23)　My father is *a doctor* and he is always *busy*.

(24)　He is *in good health*.

主語の名詞句が前置詞句の補語を指定する場合があります.

(25)　He may believe that her tiredness is *from* staying up too late last night.

(26)　The book is *about* walking.

それぞれ tiredness from … , a book about … という連鎖がもとになっていることがわかります.

## 5.3　主語の数と補語の数

(27), (28) のように, 単数主語は単数補語, 複数主語は複数補語となるのが原則です.

(27)　He *is* a great fan of Lady Gaga.

(28)　They *are* great fans of Lady Gaga.

ただし, 次の場合は複数主語でも単数補語になります.

(29) a.　補語が集合名詞の場合：We *are* a group of volunteers. / They *are* an elite family.

b.　主語が性質を表す名詞の場合：Tomatoes *are* a plant. (Tomatoes are plants. も可) / Needless emails *are* a problem.

c.　主語が総称で補語が言い換えの場合：Tulips *are* my favorite flower. (My favorite flower is tulips.)

### 5.4　第 II 文型のいろいろな構文

(30)　非人称の it の構文

 a.　*It* was *warm* enough for us to sit outside.

 b.　*It seems* that he is ill.

(31)　仮主語 it の構文

 a.　*It's pleasant* listening to American pops.

 b.　*It is* always *interesting* to hear other people's point of view.

 c.　*It is well-known* that he is a man from Zambia.

 d.　*It seems apparent* that the job is above his capability.

(32)　断定の法表現

 No, I do like Chinese food. *It's just that* I'm not hungry.

(33)　分裂文（強調構文）

 a.　*It was* yesterday *that* John came.

 b.　*It was* John *who* came yesterday.

 c.　*It was* in Cincinnati *where* they first rose to prominence.

 d.　*It was* in 2000 *when* my parents realized that my mother had Alzheimer's disease.

(34)　擬似分裂文

 a.　*What she needs is* to be left alone.

 b.　*What I want is* my own house.

 c.　*All he always said to me was* that I should continue to be humble.

## 6　第 III 文型　S V O (A)

　目的語になるものには名詞句，to 不定詞，ING（G），that 節，間接疑問節など多様な種類があるので，第 III 文型を取る動詞とその動詞型は多様です。

 (35)　You've *boiled* the eggs too long.　　　　[目的語は名詞句, too long は副詞]

(36)　She *enjoys* playing tennis.　　　　　　　　　　[目的語は動名詞]

(37)　I *forgot* to turn off the radio until next morning.

[目的語は名詞用法の to 不定詞]

(38)　I don't *know* how to go downtown.　　　[目的語は疑問詞＋to 不定詞]

(39)　I *hear* that you've been abroad.　　　　　　　[目的語は that 節]

(40)　I've *bought* some chocolate for you.

[目的語は名詞句, for you は副詞用法の前置詞句. Ｓ Ｖ Ｏ Ａ]

(41)　America *spends* a lot of money on education.

[目的語は名詞句, on … は副詞用法の前置詞句. Ｓ Ｖ Ｏ Ａ]

(42)　Please *put* the milk in the refrigerator.

[目的語は名詞句, in … は場所を表す副詞句. Ｓ Ｖ Ｏ Ａ]

(43)　The boy *hit* me on the head.

[目的語は名詞句, on the head は体の部分を表す. Ｓ Ｖ Ｏ Ａ]

(44)　He was trying to *talk* her out of doing it.

[talk は使役を表し, 目的語は名詞句 her で, out of … の前置詞句をとる. Ｓ Ｖ Ｏ Ａ]

(45)　It annoyed *her* that he could be so calm at such a time.

[目的語は名詞句 her. that 節は主語で, 仮主語 it をとっている]


## 6.1　第 III 文型をとる動詞で注意すべきもの

(46)　that 節をとる動詞

　　a.　思考や伝達の意味を持った他動詞

　　　　assume, believe, calculate, confess, confirm, consider, declare, dis-
　　　　close, estimate, feel, guess, hear, hope, know, learn, maintain, pre-
　　　　sume, prove, recognize, report, reveal, say, see, show, state, sup-
　　　　pose, think などが代表的なものです. 指示を与える意味を持った
　　　　他動詞 (demand, suggest など) も that 節をとりますが, その場合
　　　　は that 節の中は仮定法現在になります.

　　b.　自動詞＋前置詞の形をしていたものが that 節をとるために前置詞
　　　　を落とす場合

admit（to）, agree（about）, boast（about）, care（about）, complain
（about）, confess（to）, disagree（on）, gamble（on）, joke（about）,
worry（about）などがあります.

He doesn't seem to care about your feelings.

He doesn't seem to care that you abandoned him.

- c.　身振り動作を表す自動詞

  動作で伝達する内容を that 節で表現することがあります.

  Maria nodded that she understood.

- d.　object

  自動詞ですが, 反対する理由を述べる that 節を取ることがあります.

  He objected that the police had arrested him without sufficient evidence.

(47)　臨時目的語をとる動詞

swim は自動詞ですが, I can swim（the）breaststroke for an hour or
more. のように泳法を目的語に取る場合があります.「平泳ぎをする」
は do（the）breaststroke とも言うので, この例の swim も他動詞に
なっています. これは特別な用法で, このような（the）breaststroke
を臨時目的語（ad hoc object）と言います.

(48)　人＋身体部位の形をとる動詞

The doctor looked me in the eye. のように, 身体の全体を先に述べて,
それから行為の対象先である身体部位を前置詞句で追加する形です.

(49)　同族目的語をとる動詞

He died a tragic death. のように自動詞が同じ意味を表す派生名詞を
取る形があり, これを同族目的語構文（cognate object construction）
と言います. 他には smile a faint smile, live a happy life などという
形があります.

(50)　説得・脅迫動詞の使役動詞化

make, have などの本来的な使役動詞とは別に, talk や persuade, in-
timidate といった動詞は「説得して人に…させる, させない」「脅した
り誘惑したりして人に…させる」といった使役的な意味を表すことが

あります．これらは迂言的使役動詞（periphrastic causative verb）と呼ばれ，「動詞＋目的語＋into/out of ...」という形を取ります．この形に使えるものは argue, cheat, frighten, order, persuade, stimulate といった説得や行為を表すものや，bully, deceive, entice, intimate といった誘惑や脅迫を表すものがあります．

# 7　第 IV 文型　S V O O

give に代表される，人に物や情報などを与えることを意味する動詞は目的語を 2 つとります（二重目的語動詞）．(52), (53) を見てください．与えられるものが情報の場合は名詞句のほか that 節や wh 節でも表現されます．このような二重目的語構文は，(51), (52), (53) のように単に物・情報の移動を表す場合と (54) のように恩恵を与えることを意味する場合があります．

(51)　Have they *paid* you the money?

(52)　They *informed* me that Mr. Raiden has been elected President of the EU Council.

(53)　*Tell* me what your name is.

(54)　Mother *made* me a good cup of coffee.

移動を表す場合は，to 前置詞句を使用した第 III 文型で表現できる場合があります．

(55)　We *gave* a lot of money **to** his campaign.

to をとる動詞には，bring, carry, give, hand, lend, offer, pass, sell, show, throw などがあります．

恩恵を表す場合は，for 前置詞句を使用した第 III 文型で表現できる場合があります．上記の (54) もそうです．この (54) の「…のために」の意味になるような間接目的語を「利害の与格」（dative of interest）と呼ぶこともあります．

(56)　Tom's parents *bought* a new laptop **for** him.

for をとる動詞には，bring, buy, get, order, pour などがあります．

両方とることができる動詞がありますが，意味が異なることに注意しましょう．

(57) a.　The restaurant will *bring* it **to** you as you order.

　　 b.　She was nice enough to *bring* it **for** you.

第 IV 文型をとっても，第 III 文型にならない動詞があります．cause, charge, cost, deny, envy, promise, wish などです．

(58) a.　The restaurant *charged* us ￡40 for the wine. (×… charged ￡40 to/for/on us.)

　　 b.　I *wish* you good luck. (×I wish good luck to/for you.)

# 8　第 V 文型　S V O C

## 8.1　O C に見られる主述関係

第 V 文型では，O と C の関係が主語と述語の関係にあります．

(59)　He *boiled* **the eggs** too **hard**. (The eggs were too hard.)

(60)　We *believe* **him to be** the finest violinist in the world. (He is the finest violinist in the world.)

(61)　They *think* **it odd** that he's back from lunch at this early hour. (It is odd that he's back …)

(62)　They *saw* **someone coming** down the road. (Someone is coming down the road.)

(63)　They *expect* **you to come** to every class on time. (You come to every class on time.)

(64)　He couldn't understand what they were saying and *make* **himself**

**understood**. (He was understood.)

(65)　*Stop* **them taking** photos. (They are taking photos.)

　(59) の例では，卵をゆでた結果生じた状態を表しているのが補語の hard で
す（ゆでた結果，卵が固くなった）．このような結果を表す形を結果構文（resul-
tative construction）と呼ぶことがあります．結果構文では I'll kill you dead./I
pressed the program flat on the table. のように，いろいろな動詞が使われます．

　believe, expect, find, think, know, understand などの動詞は，that 節をとる第
III 文型との対応関係を持つものもあります．(66) の例で対応関係を確認してく
ださい．

(66)　a.　The police *believed* that the Mafia had committed the crime.

　　　b.　The police *believed* the Mafia to have committed the crime.


## ＜もっと詳しく＞　　☞ 『**現代高等英文法**』 p. 77
「仮目的語をとる形，仮目的語を省略する形」


## 8.2　第 V 文型をとるいろいろな動詞

(67)　命名動詞 (naming verb)：call, name などです．
　　　We *call* her Liz.

(68)　知覚動詞 (perception verb)
　　　see, feel, hear, notice, watch などです．一部の知覚動詞は受動形にす
　　　ると to 不定詞を取ります．
　　a.　I *saw* him coming out of Johnsons' house.
　　b.　I *saw* him go to the lake and kneel down.
　　c.　I *saw* him arrested in front of my eyes.
　　d.　He *was seen to* leave a few minutes ago.

(69)　意思動詞 (verb of intention)
　　　ask, expect, hate, want, wish などです．《米》では目的語の前に for を
　　　取る場合があります．

    a.   They *asked* him to leave.

    b.   I *want* you to listen and tell me what you think.

    c.   We *wish for* you to come to the house tonight.

(70)   使役動詞 (causative verb)

    let, make, have, get などです.

    a.   *Make* him go whether he likes or not.

    b.   *Let* him go if he wants to.

    c.   I'm going to *get* the barber to cut my hair this afternoon.

    d.   I'm going to *get* my hair cut this afternoon.

(71)   V O ING (P) をとるもの

    catch, keep, leave, prevent, save, stop などです.

    He *caught* me looking and I pretended I was watching TV.


# 9　動作と状態

　動詞の表す意味によって,動作 (dynamic) か状態 (stative) を区別する必要があります. この意味的な区別は,自らの意志で行為を行うことができるかどうかといった観点から考えます. この意味的な区別は,その動詞を命令形にできるか,進行形にできるか,継続を表す完了形にした際に進行形にするかどうかといったことに関係します. ただし,状態動詞を進行形にした I'm loving it. のような例もありますが,くだけた会話で使用されます.

(72) a.  *Study* English harder.  [動作]

     b.  ×*Know* English more.  [状態]

(73) a.  They *are having* a good time.  [動作]

     b.  He *has* a book in his hand.  [状態]

        (×He *is having* a book in his hand.)

(74) a.  I'll *be seeing* you tomorrow.  [動作]

     b.  We *see* a lot of stars.  [状態]( ×We *are seeing* a lot of stars now.)

(75) a.　They *have known* each other for ten years.　[状態]

　　 b.　Tom *has been reading* the book for three hours.　[動作]

　　　　 (×Tom *has read* the book for three hours.)

# 10　群動詞

　動詞といくつかの他の要素からなりたつ動詞のフレーズを，群動詞と呼びます．群動詞にはそれぞれの成り立ちに応じて，以下のようなものがあります．

Table 2.1.3　群動詞の成り立ちと例

| | 成り立ち | 例 |
|---|---|---|
| 句動詞 (phrasal verb) | 動詞＋副詞 | put off, fill out など |
| 前置詞動詞 (prepositional verb) | 動詞＋前置詞 | lead to, wait for など |
| 句前置詞動詞<br>(phrasal-prepositional verb) | 動詞＋副詞＋前置詞 | look forward to など |
| 複合動詞 (compound verb) | 動詞＋$\alpha$／$\alpha$＋動詞 | hitch-hike など |
| イディオム動詞 (idiomatic verb) | 動詞＋名詞＋前置詞 | take care of など |

## 10.1　句動詞

　(76) から (81) の例に示すように，句動詞は，「動詞＋副詞」がひとまとまりになり，ひとつの動詞の機能を果たします．口語的な表現で，別のひとつの動詞に置き換えることができるものもあります．他動詞的な句動詞は (80) の例やNobody should be left out. のように，受身になることもできます．

(76)　We had to *put off* the meeting until the next day.　( ＝postpone)

(77)　Before beginning classes, each student must *fill out* many forms.　( ＝complete)

(78)　He felt *let down* when he heard the news.　( ＝disappoint)

(79)　I'll *put* you *down* for the London tour. ( = book)

(80)　Anyone who interrupts will be *put out*. ( = expel)

(81)　He *threw up* after eating too much. ( = vomit)

　また，副詞要素は時によって名詞の前にも後にも置けますが，次節の前置詞動詞との違いに注意しましょう.

(82)　[句動詞] I *threw away* my old briefcase. ⇄ I *threw* my old brief-case *away*.

(83)　[前置詞動詞] I'm *looking for* it. ( ×I'm *looking* it *for*.)

ただし，句動詞の場合でも，名詞が代名詞の場合は副詞をその後に置きます.

(84)　*Put* it *out*! （火を消して！）( ×*Put out* it.)


## 10.2　前置詞動詞

　前置詞動詞は，動詞＋前置詞がひとまとまりになっています.「動詞＋前置詞＋名詞」の形になるもの ( = (85), (86), (87))，「動詞＋名詞＋前置詞＋名詞」の形になるもの ( = (88), (89)) があります.

(85)　I don't *care for* coffee.

(86)　All roads *lead to* Rome.

(87)　All we can do is *wait for* him.

(88)　No one would *blame* you *for* a genuine mistake.

(89)　His child's illness *put* him *through* the wringer.

　表面上は似ていても，前置詞動詞なのか，動詞＋前置詞句の別の表現なのかを区別する必要があります.前置詞句が副詞で置き換えられるかどうかがひとつの基準になります.

(90)　He *lives in* Tokyo. ( = He lives there.)　　　　　　　　[動詞＋前置詞句]

(91)　The burglar *broke in* the house. ( ×The burglar broke there.)

[前置詞動詞]

前置詞動詞全体が他動詞的になり，受動態にできる場合があります．

(92)　He *was laughed at* when he made that ridiculous mistake.

## 10.3　句前置詞動詞

「自動詞＋副詞＋前置詞」が結合して成句になっているものを句前置詞動詞といい，put up with や look forward to, sit in for などがあります．全体としてひとつの動詞になっており，これらも意味的に類似した動詞に置き換えることができるものがあります．

(93)　The student *broke in on* the conversation without waiting for the speaker to stop talking. (＝interfere with)

(94)　We *look up to* him as a pioneer. (＝respect)

目的語を取っているので，時に受動態になる場合があります．

(95)　She *is looked up to* for what she has accomplished.

## 10.4　複合動詞

複合動詞には hitch-hike, ice-skate, ad-lib のようなものがあります．

(96)　It is not wise to *hitch-hike* on your own.

(97)　Children *ice-skated* on the sidewalks.

## 10.5　イディオム動詞

イディオム動詞は「動詞＋名詞＋前置詞」からなり，全体として他動詞的な働きをします．

(98)　Our family is *taking care of* a bed-ridden old person.

(99)　It is very easy to *find fault with* the work of others.

(100)　I *took advantage of* the special sale and bought a half dozen new shirts.

(101)　My parents *made light of* my worry and told me to *take no notice of* what people said.

受身にする際には，イディオム動詞を構成する名詞を主語にする場合と，前置詞の目的語を主語にする場合があります．

(102)　Make sure that my father will *be taken care of.*

(103)　We found *little care was taken of* the house.

# ◉練習問題◉

1　動詞の ask は，どのような意味でどのような文型，動詞型で使用されるかを辞書で調べなさい.

_____

_____

_____

_____

_____

_____

_____

_____

2　イタリック部分の群動詞を他の動詞で言い換えなさい.

2.1　"Tell your friend to *go away*." "I can't." _____

2.2　I raised him after his mother and father *passed away*. _____

2.3　"*Cut it out*!" _____

2.4　They didn't expect the Olympics to be *put off* until 2021.

_____

2.5　She *filled out* the application form and asked a lot of questions.

_____

2.6　I won't *let* you *down*.　_____

2.7　Most of the business leaders never *took to* the new president.

_____

2.8　I'm convinced Suzie will always *stand by* me when trouble happens.

_____

2.9　This *got* me *through* the hardest time of my life.　_____

2.10　She is a politician to be *looked up to*.　_____

2.11　Give me some tips to *cut back on* sugar in my diet.　_____

2.12　Some scientists argue that our moon might *be made up of* many smaller moons.　_____

## 3　Oral translation: 以下の日本語を英語にしなさい.

3.1　私は自分の計画を誰にも邪魔させない. (allow / interfere を使って)

_____

3.2　どうしてすぐに携帯メールの返事をくれなかったのですか.

_____

3.3　一郎に電話してみたらと, メアリーに提案してみました. (suggest を使って)

_____

3.4　あなたが一緒に行ってくれるといいのですが. (wish を使って)

_____

3.5　その T シャツは君に似合うね. どこで買ったの.

_____

3.6　お腹がすいているときは何でもおいしい.

_____

3.7　海外旅行中は特に健康には注意しなさい. (look out for を使って)

_____

3.8　私はその件とは何の関係もありません. いろいろと聞かれるのは迷惑です.

_____

3.9　近頃は交通も便利になり，田舎に帰るのもそれほどおっくうではなくなった．（don't feel it a big bother to do を使って）

_____

3.10　リサイクルだけではプラスチックごみは減らせない．（get rid of を使って）

_____

3.11　のどが渇いた．何か冷たいものをください．

_____

3.12　彼女は私を離してくれませんでした．

_____

3.13　私は彼に私の電話番号の書いてある名刺を手渡した．

_____

# 第2章　時制と相

（『現代高等英文法』pp. 89 〜 117 に該当）

## 1　時制と相

### 1.1　時制

(1) The old man *takes* the dog for a walk every morning. 　　　［現在時制］

(2) The Prime Minister *flew* into New York yesterday to start her visit to the U.S. 　　　［過去時制］

(3) My father *will* probably *be* in hospital for at least two weeks. ［未来時制］

時制（tense）とは，「話し手の発話時」と「話題になっている出来事」の時間関係を動詞の変化形で表すものです．定形節の文では必ず時制が表現されます．

時制は動詞の変化形で表されますので，英語の基本時制として（1）の例の現在時制（present tense）と（2）の例の過去時制（past tense）を認めることができます．動詞は未来を表すための特別な変化形を持たないので，英語に未来時制（future tense）を認めるかどうかは文法家によって異なりますが，本書では（3）の will ＋主動詞という形で未来時制を認める立場を取ります．

### 1.2　相

相（aspect）とは，現在・過去・未来において，動詞の表す行為が継続しているか，完了しているかを表す文法上のしくみを言います．英語の相には進行相と完了相のふたつがあります．

(4) I never read classics and now I'*m reading* them. [現在進行形]

(5) The children *were fighting* all morning. [過去進行形]

(6) There's no telling what we'*ll be seeing* soon. [未来進行形]

(7) They *have been* unhappy for a long time. [現在完了形]

(8) We *had heard* a lot about her before we ever met her. [過去完了形]

(9) We'*ll have finished* the building work by next month. [未来完了形]

## 1.3　時制と相の組み合わせ

　時制と相の組み合わせは以下の通りになります．完了進行形として組み合わせる際の相の順番は，完了相が先，進行相が後になります．

Table 2.2.1　時制と相の組み合わせ

| 時制 | 完了相 | 進行相 | | | |
|---|---|---|---|---|---|
| 現在 | | | → | 現在形 | write / writes |
| 現在 | | ✔ | → | 現在進行形 | is / are writing |
| 現在 | ✔ | | → | 現在完了形 | has / have written |
| 現在 | ✔ | ✔ | → | 現在完了進行形 | has / have been writing |
| 過去 | | | → | 過去形 | wrote |
| 過去 | | ✔ | → | 過去進行形 | was / were writing |
| 過去 | ✔ | | → | 過去完了形 | had written |
| 過去 | ✔ | ✔ | → | 過去完了進行形 | had been writing |
| 未来 | | | → | 未来形 | will write |
| 未来 | | ✔ | → | 未来進行形 | will be writing |
| 未来 | ✔ | | → | 未来完了形 | will have written |
| 未来 | ✔ | ✔ | → | 未来完了進行形 | will have been writing |

## 2　現在時制

単純な現在時制は，以下のような用法を持っています．

(10)　The dog *is* in the house.　　　　　　　　　　[現在の状態を表す]

(11)　Whenever I travel, I *get* constipation.　　　　　[習慣を表す]

(12)　Two and two *makes* [《時に》*make*] four.　　　[普遍的真理を表す]

(13)　Here you *go.* / Here *comes* the bus.　　[目の前の出来事を描写する]

(14)　I *take* three eggs and *beat* them in this bowl.　[実演しながら説明する]

(15)　I *accept* your offer.

[発言することである行為を実行する（発話行為（performative））]

(10) のような状態動詞と異なり，動作動詞の場合，単純な現在時制を使って現在の動作を表すには文脈が必要です．He always *says,* "Whatever will happen will happen."（彼の口癖は「なるようになる」だ）のように習慣を表す場合や，芝居のト書きの場合などがあります．

　過去に起こったことでも，その内容が発話時においても正しいことを伝えたい場合や，情報を活き活きとして伝えたい場合は現在形を用いることがあります．

(16)　Wife of Canada's Prime Minister *Tests* Positive for Virus

[新聞の見出しで]

(17)　The forecast *says* it's going to be gorgeous today.　　[ニュースで]

(18)　I was just about to go to bed when all of a sudden there's a knock at the door and Sam *rushes* in.　　　　[歴史的現在]

(17) を The forecast said … と過去時制で述べることも可能ですが，その場合は伝達内容が発話時でも正しいかどうかについて発話者は関知しません．

　未来のことでも次の場合は現在形を用います．

(19)　Christmas day *falls* on a Thursday this year.　　[確定未来を表す]

(20)　Let me know as soon as he *comes.* [時の副詞節の中で未来のことを言う]

(21)   If you *feel* seasick, take one of those pills.

[条件の副詞節で未来のことを言う]

(20) や (21) のような副詞節を導くものには when, after, before, as, if, as soon as, once, in case などがあります.


# 3   過去時制

過去時制は，過去の状態や動作を述べるのに使われます ((22), (23) が該当).
また，過去形は発話者が発話している今と時間的距離を置くことになるので，発話者との距離を置く「丁寧さ」を表す用法を持ちます. また，仮定法過去形構文でも使われます ((25) が該当).

(22)   I *was* a member of the tennis club of my college. [過去の状態を述べる]
(23)   He *got up* from the table carrying the pie in his fingers.

[過去に行った動作を述べる]
(24)   *Did* you wish to look at our higher-priced shoes?   [丁寧な表現にする]
(25)   He talks as if he *owned* the place.

[現在の事実と反する内容を述べる（仮定法過去形構文）]

伝達動詞が導く節の中では，伝達動詞の過去形に合わせて節内の動詞も過去形にします（時制の一致 (tense shift)）.

(26) a.   I *didn't* realize that the match *started* tomorrow.
     b.   I *didn't* realize that the match *would* start tomorrow.
(27) a.   Columbus *believed* the earth *was* round.
     b.   She *said* she *feels* good now.

(26a) では，The match starts tomorrow. という確定未来を表す現在形が時制の一致を受けています. (26b) では The match will start tomorrow. が時制の一致を受けています. The earth is round. は今でも正しいので (27) では時制の一致

の必要がないように感じますが，ここではコロンブスの信念や考えたことを述べているので過去形になっています．（27b）では過去に彼女が述べた内容は，発話時でもそうであるということを示すために，時制の一致をさせずに現在時制のままになっています．

　過去形が完了形の代用をすることがあります．

(28)　*Did* you ever hear of such a thing?

[現在までの経験を述べる現在完了形の代用]

(29)　The bus *started* just before I reached the bus stop.

[過去より前の出来事を述べる過去完了形の代用]

　(30) のように，since が導く節内では過去形が使われます．また，（31）の例では，主節が過去完了なので，when 節内も過去完了になると思うかもしれませんが，この when 節は ten years ago などと同じように具体的な過去の時間を指定するものですので，過去形になります．

(30)　It's been years since I *saw* him last.

(31)　His mind drifted to a building he'd often gazed at when he *was* younger.

## ＜もっと詳しく＞　☞『**現代高等英文法**』p. 97
「since 節内の時制・相と主節の時制・相の関係」

## 4　未来時制

　「will / shall ＋原形」によって未来のことを表すことができます．未来のことは，他にも現在時制や現在進行形でも表すことができます．

(32)　Jane *will be* sixteen tomorrow.　　　　　[単純未来を表す]

(33)　If I see him, I'*ll tell* him exactly what I think of him.　　[意志未来]

(34)　I *shall* certainly *miss* you when you go back to New Zealand.《英》

[単純未来]

will / shall の代用表現として，be going to, be to, be about to などがあります．

(35)　Molly's *going to* have another baby in June.　　　　　[単純未来]

(36)　They *are to* be married in June.　　　　　　　　　　[単純未来]


# 5　完了形

## 5.1　現在完了形

　現在完了形（present perfect）は，過去の行為・出来事あるいは過去に始まった
行為・出来事が，発話時点（現在）まで影響していることを表現します．動詞の種
類や時を表す副詞によって，完了，継続，経験の 3 つの意味が顕著になります．

(37)　a.　I'*ve* just *finished* reading a fantastic book and I'd love you to read
　　　　　it.　[完了]

　　　b.　Winter *has gone* and spring *has come*.　[完了]

(38)　a.　My father *has been* sick for over a month.　[継続]

　　　b.　She *has played* piano with the New York Philharmonic for the
　　　　　past ten years.　[継続]

(39)　Humans *have been* to the moon.　[経験]

動作動詞でも，職業や習慣的な行為を表す場合は（38b）のように継続の意味に
なります．

　live, stand, lie, sit wait, sleep などの人の動作・状態を表す動詞は，動作と状
態の中間的な意味になるので，現在完了と現在完了進行形の意味の区別が難しく
なります．次の例はほとんど同じ意味で使われます．

(40)　a.　I *have sat* here for over two hours.

　　　b.　I *have been sitting* here for over two hours.

それぞれの意味で使われる動詞の種類と共起する典型的副詞を Table 2.2.2 に

まとめました.

Table 2.2.2　完了形の表す意味と共起する動詞・副詞の特徴

| 意味 | 動詞の種類 | 共起する典型的副詞 |
|---|---|---|
| 完了 | 動作動詞 | just, already などの副詞 |
| 継続 | 状態動詞，習慣的動作を表す動詞 | 期間を表す for a week などの副詞 |
| 経験 | 繰り返し行える動作を表す動詞 | 回数・開始の時を表す副詞，ever, never など |

　以下，それぞれの意味を図示したものを見ながら，過去の状態や出来事が現在に影響を与えていることを理解してください. ここでは●が発話時，○が動作，=== が状態，→は時間の流れを表します.

(41) The show *has* just *been* cancelled.（ショーの会場のアナウンス）[完了]
ショーのキャンセルがアナウンスの直前に決められたことを表しています. 「今日はショーを見られませんよ」というような現在への影響・余韻が残ります.

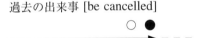

過去の出来事 [be cancelled]

(42) My father *has been* sick for over ten years. 　[継続]
10 年以上前からの状態が発話時まで継続しています.

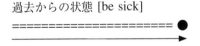

過去からの状態 [be sick]

(43) He *has played* baseball for four years. 　[継続]
play baseball という行為が発話時まで繰り返されています.

ある行為 [play baseball]

(44)　My mom *has been* dead since I was ten.　[継続]

My mom died という行為の結果状態 (be dead) が発話時まで継続しています.

ある行為 [die]　結果状態　[be dead]

(45)　I *have visited* Paris twice.　[経験]

過去から発話時まで同種の行為を何度か行っています.

ある行為 [visit Paris]

これらの図が示すように, 現在完了は発話時現在を含んだ事象を表しているので, 過去を表す表現とは一緒に使うことはできません. when も過去の時を聞く場合は現在完了とともに用いませんが, 現在まで影響を残す過去の経験を問う場合に使われることがあります.

(46)　*When have* you ever *been* in this situation before?

（これまでにいつこんな状況になりましたか）

次の文を比較して過去形との違いを理解しましょう.

(47)　a.　I *haven't had* breakfast this morning. （まだ朝食を食べていない）

[発話しているのは今朝]

　　　b.　I *didn't have* breakfast this morning. （今朝は朝食を食べなかった）

[午後以後の発話]

have been to は (39) で示したように, 経験の意味を表しますが, 次の例のように just などを伴って「行ってきたところです」（今帰ってきましたという余韻）を表すことがあります.

(48)　I *have just been* to a burial this morning.

古い英語には「be 動詞＋過去分詞」で完了を表す用法がありました．その名残が現代英語のいくつかの表現に残っています．*Are* you *finished*?（（レストランなどで）もうおすみですか）というのがそれです．他に I'*m done*. や She'*s gone*.（She's＝She is）などもその用法です．


## 5.2 過去完了形

過去完了形（past perfect）は，現在完了形が過去になって，過去の完了，経験，継続の意味を表します（(49), (50), (51)）．また，過去からみてさらに過去（大過去（pluperfect））を表す用法を持っています（(52)）．過去の事実と反することを述べる仮定法過去完了でも使用します（(53)）．

(49) When I came back to London, winter *had* already *gone*.

[完了を表す現在完了の過去]

(50) My father *had been* sick for over a month before he recovered his health again. [継続を表す現在完了の過去]

(51) The child *had* not *seen* her father since she was one year old.

[経験を表す現在完了の過去]

(52) I woke up just before ten and went down to the second floor. My mother *had* already *left* for work. [大過去]
（目を覚ましたという過去の出来事の前に母親が出かけていた）

(53) If I *had gone* to university, I would have studied medicine.

[仮定法過去完了]

上の例のように，過去完了では基準になる過去時が明示されることが多いのですが，文脈から基準の過去時を補うような場合は，それが明示されない時があります．次の例では文脈から「この前彼女に会ったときに」というような基準時が了解されているのです．

(54) Her hair *had* not *lost* its ripe nut color.

過去の計画の変更を表す場合や，過去の願望が実現されなかったことを表す場

合に過去完了形が使われます.

(55)　I *had planned* to work till I was sixty but I can't any more.

(56)　I *had hoped* to catch the 8:30 train but found it was gone.

scarcely/hardly A when/before/than B の構文では A の節に過去完了形が現れます.

(57)　She *had* hardly *arrived* when she started talking about leaving again.

A の次に B が起こる場合, A before B か after A, B となりますが, 時間的に見て A が先に起こっているのでどちらの場合も A が過去完了になるのが基本です. 取り立てて過去完了にしなくても前後関係は明らかなので, A, B ともに過去形になることもあります.

(58)　After she *had become* Queen, she soon went to visit her parents in Leeds.

(59)　After she *became* ill he stopped seeing her.

A before B の時に B に過去完了形がくることがあります. これは「…してしまわないうちに」という完了の意味を表しますが, 過去形との違いは必ずしも明確ではありません.

(60)　They destroyed the letter before I *read* it.（読む前に）

(61)　They destroyed the letter before I *had read* it.
　　　（読んでもいないのに / 読み終わらないうちに）

現在完了形, 過去形が時制の一致を受けて過去完了形になるときもあります.

(62)　The doctor told her how badly she *had been* injured.
　　　(You were so badly injured. が伝達内容)

(63)　The king saw that he *had lost* the whole kingdom.
　　　(I have lost the whole kingdom. が伝達内容)

## 5.3 未来完了形

未来完了形 (future perfect) は，未来のある時に行為や状態が完了しているか，継続しているか，何度それを経験しているかということを表現します．

(64) By the end of this season, he *will have made* about $170 million playing baseball. [完了]

(65) a. Next year we *will have known* each other for 75 years. [状態の継続]

b. "I *will have sung* for 56 years." [動作の継続]

((デビューから) 56年間歌い続けることになります)

(66) Many people *will have tried* one or more home remedies before they seek professional help for insomnia. [経験]

発話時に起こっている動作や状態に対する未来の評価を予測して言う場合にも未来完了形が使われます．

(67) He *will not have died* in vain.

((すでに亡くなっている人に対して) 彼の死は無駄にしない)

# 6 進行形

## 6.1 現在進行形

現在進行形 (present progressive) は，行為が継続することを表します．継続を表す場合，動詞の意味に応じて，「動作を…している」(継続)，「徐々に…している」(状態変化)，「動作を繰り返し…している」(反復行為)，「…しつつある」(未完了) を意味します．状態動詞を進行形にすると一時性を強調します．また，現在進行形は丁寧さを表す用法や近接未来を表す用法を持っています．

(68) I'*m making* breakfast. [継続]

(69) He's been in hospital for three weeks but *is improving* steadily.

[進行中の状態変化]

(70)   He *is knocking* quietly on the old door.                [反復行為]

(71)   I'*m seeing* her quite a bit right now.                [反復行為]

(72)   The rain *is stopping*.                [未完了]

(73)   Mary *is living* with her parents now.        [一時的状態]

(74)   *Are* you *wanting* a muffin, Peter?                [丁寧]

(75)   Abe and Mary *are leaving* next Monday.        [近接未来]

(72) のように，die, stop, などのある結果状態へ向かう行為を表現する完結動詞 (conclusive verb) が進行形になると未完了の意味になります．発着往来を表す動詞 (arrive, leave, land) は，状況によって，未完了，近接未来，繰り返しの事態を表します．

(76) a.   Hurry! The taxi *is arriving*.        [未完了]（まもなく着く）

b.   My wife and I *are arriving* separately.        [近接未来]

c.   Guests *are arriving*. Help me greet them.

[繰り返し]（次々に到着する）

be 動詞は状態を表すので，その進行形は (73) と同じように一時的な状態の意味になります．

(77)   I don't think we *are being* silly. (ふざけたことをしているとは思いません)

have to は進行形でいらだちなどの感情を表すことがあります．

(78)   I'*m having* to take care of patients at all hours of the day and night.

## 6.2   過去進行形

過去進行形 (past progressive) は，基本的に現在進行形を過去形にしたものです．また，仮定法過去の進行形もあります．

(79)   The phone rang while I *was having* dinner. [出来事の背景的状況の説明]

(80)   She *was* always *complaining* about watching her own grandchild.

[反復行為]

(81)　I *was wondering* if I could use the credit card to get my computer fixed.　　　　　　　　　　　　　　　　　　　　　［丁寧］

(82)　I wouldn't have to be here if you *were doing* your job properly.

　　　　　　　　　　　　　　　　　　　　　　［仮定法過去進行形］

## 6.3　未来進行形

　未来進行形（future progressive）は，未来の行動を予測したり，近い未来の行為を述べたり，未来での行為の継続を述べたりします．

(83)　With the onset of autumn, these animals *will be looking* for food more aggressively.　　　　　　　　　　［未来の行動の予測］

(84) a.　I'*ll be leaving* for Hong Kong tomorrow.　　［近い未来の行為］

　　 b.　I'*ll be seeing* you soon.　　　　　　　　　　［近い未来の行為］

(85)　Mary *will be working* on the assignment for a month.

　　　　　　　　　　　　　　　　　　　　　　［未来での行為の継続］

単純な未来形でも予定を表現できますが，(84)のように未来進行形にすることで人の意志や予定の意味を薄め，自然とそうなるかのように表現して丁寧さを出しています．

## 7　完了進行形

　現在完了進行形（present perfect progressive）は，発話時（現在）に至るまでの行為の継続を言います．進行形はまだ行為が終わっていないということを表すので，現在完了進行形と現在完了形とでは対照的な意味の違いがあります．

(86) a.　I'*ve cleaned* the windows.　　　　　　　［完了］（拭き終わった）

　　 b.　I'*ve been cleaning* the windows.

　　　　　　　　　　　　　［行為の継続］（まだ拭き終わっていない）

動作動詞の現在完了形と期間を表す副詞は共起できませんが, 現在完了進行形では可能になります. これは進行形のもつ継続の意味からくる違いです.

(87)   They*'ve been repairing* the road for months.

  (×They*'ve repaired* the road for months.)

また, 動作動詞の場合は, 単純な完了形が職業や習慣的行為の継続を表し, 現在完了進行形の場合は別の意味で動作を継続しているということを表す場合があります. この場合, 単純な完了形でも期間を表す副詞句と共起できます. これは習慣的な行為が継続していることを表すためです. 次の2つの文の work の意味の違いに注意しましょう.

(88) a.   Joe Wilson *has worked* in the loan industry for over two decades.

[職業や習慣的行為の継続]

b.   Ebony *has been working* to develop her capability as a poet.

[取り組むという動作の継続]

現在完了進行形は, 何かの証拠が今も残っていることを含意する場合があります. (89) を見てみましょう.

(89) a.   You*'ve been fighting* again.

  ((あざができているなどして) またけんかしてたね)

b.   *Have* you *been crying*? ((目が赤いなどの理由から) 泣いていたの)

過去完了進行形 (past perfect progressive) は, 過去の特定の時までの行為の継続を言います. また仮定法過去完了でも進行形になることがあります.

(90)   Karen *had been working* hard, so her doctor told her to take a vacation. She *had been trying* to finish her degree that year.

  (医者に会うまでのカレンの継続的な行為)

(91)   He would never have been driving that car if he *had been drinking*.

[仮定法過去完了進行形]

未来完了進行形 (future perfect progressive) は, 使用される頻度は高くあり

ません．未来のある時点での行為の継続を表現しますが，その期間の長さに焦点
が当てられます．

(92)　By six o'clock they *will have been meeting* for almost ten hours.

(93)　In March, I *will have been living* with Schmidt for ten years.


# ●練習問題●

1　次の各文のかっこの中の選択肢の中から，適切な時制・相表現を選びなさい．

1.1　I (am going / go) to university by train every day.

1.2　When he came back home, he told his wife that he (had been / is) in the
library a couple of hours waiting for his friend.

1.3　"What's up, Mike?" "What (do you do / are you doing) here, John?"

1.4　He is not, and never (will have been / has been) my friend.

1.5　Just relax. (I'm not being / I have not been) spiteful.

1.6　My wife (will be joining / joined) us in a moment.

1.7　When her father died, she (has finally been / was finally) persuaded to
move to a new house.

1.8　They (have been / are) happy together for over forty years since they got
married.

1.9　In the 1990s, when I was a university student, I thought I (would / will)
be a psychologist, and (had headed / headed) into a Ph.D. program at the
University of X.

1.10　We'll give you instructions before you (will start / start).

1.11　"Are you with me?" "(I was / I'm) all ears."

1.12　If he (will ask / asks), don't tell him.

1.13　As soon as they went out of the room, I (turned / have turned) to face
him and asked, "What was that about?"

1.14　I still (have / am having) the data on my laptop.

1.15 "See you in a year or so." "By then, I (am traveling / will have traveled) around the world.

1.16 If they (had known / knew) what the message meant, they would have left the room right away.

## 2　Oral translation: 以下の日本文を英語にしなさい.

2.1　「雨降ってる?」「うん, 少し降ってるよ」

_____

2.2　あいつは今日 1 時に来ると言っていたのにまだ来ない.

_____

2.3　僕が来るまで君は何をしてたの.

_____

2.4　窓から富士山が見えてます.

_____

2.5　今日は朝食に何を食べましたか.

_____

2.6　教室に入ると先生がもう来ていて驚いた.

_____

2.7　毎年たくさんの観光客が奈良を訪れます.

_____

2.8　来年カナダに行ったら 5 回目になる.

_____

2.9　スマートフォンが登場してコミュニケーションがより早くできるように
　　なった.

_____

2.10 国連のレポートは, 適切な手段を取らなければ気候変動が悪化すると警告
　　しています.

_____

# 第3章　助動詞

(『現代高等英文法』pp. 118 〜 149 に該当)

## 1　助動詞

### 1.1　助動詞の種類

　助動詞（auxiliary verb）には，主動詞を補助する機能を果たす一般助動詞（general auxiliary verb）と法助動詞（modal auxiliary）があります．Table 2.3.1 を見てください．(2) 等は用例番号を指します．

Table 2.3.1　助動詞の種類

| 一般助動詞 | | be（受動態を作る）<br>have（完了形を作る）<br>do（疑問文・否定文を作る，動詞の強調） | (2),<br>(3),<br>(4),<br>(5),<br>(6) |
|---|---|---|---|
| 法助動詞 | 主要法助動詞（principal modal auxiliary） | will, would, shall, should, can, could, may, might, must, *dare, *need | (7)<br>以降 |
| | 準法助動詞（semi-modal auxiliary） | be going to, be to, be about to, have to, be able to, used to | |

＊ dare, need にはそれぞれ動詞用法があるため，準法助動詞（PART II 第 6 章）の箇所で説明します．

　法助動詞は，事実として述べられた事柄に対する話し手の気持ちを表します．(1) の例に見るように，can を使うと「He swims very well. ということが，話

し手である私にとって可能であると思える」ということを表します.

(1)　He *can* swim very well.

(2)〜(5) は一般助動詞としての, (6) は動詞としての do の用法を示しています.

(2) a.　I *don*'t work on Saturdays.　[否定]

　　 b.　*Do* you come from a large family?　[疑問]

　　 c.　Why *don*'t you try them on?　[否定疑問]

(3) a.　"You *did*n't call me last night."

　　　　"I *did* call you!"　[強調]

　　 b.　Love, love me *do*.　(Beatles)　[強調]

　　 c.　Not only *does* she speak Spanish, she's good with computers.

(4)　Q: *Do* you know her?　[助動詞の do]

　　　A: Yes, I *do*./No, I *don*'t. (do = know her)　[代動詞の do]

(5) a.　"I missed the train this morning." "I've *done* that, too."

　　　　[代動詞の do. have done that = have missed the train]

　　 b.　"If you haven't finished the homework, *do* it [do so] at once."

　　　　[代動詞の do. do it/do so = finish the homework]

(6)　Have you *done* your homework?　[動詞]

## ＜もっと詳しく＞　☞『現代高等英文法』p. 121

「代動詞 do が目的語 (it, so, that) を伴う場合の意味の違い」

## 1.2　法助動詞

### 1.2.1　will の用法

(7) の例を見てください.

(7) a.　I *will* come as soon as I've finished writing the letter.　[意思未来]

　　 b.　Tomorrow *will* be a better day.　　　　　　　　　　　　[単純未来]

 c. *Will* you shut the door?         [命令]

 d. You *will* not mention this meeting to anyone.   [命令]

 e. *Will* you have a cup of tea?        [誘い]

 f. You'*ll* have had dinner already, I suppose.   [推量]

 g. On a Friday night we'*ll* get a take-away and we'*ll* just relax.

                    [習性・習慣]

 h. Natural rubber *will* stretch easily when pulled.  [習性・習慣]

 助動詞 will は，(7a, b) のように，意思未来や単純未来の意味で使われるほかにもいろいろな意味で使われます．if 節中で未来の意味の will は使われませんので注意してください．(7c) のように，Will you ...? で文末のイントネーションを下降調にすると，「…してくれる？」の意味になり，相手に対して苛立ちを持った状況での命令を表します．これを Will you *please* ...? としても丁寧な表現にはならず，さらに (7d) は相手に威圧を与える命令になるので注意が必要です．丁寧な表現としては Would you please ...? あるいはより丁寧な Could you ...? などがあります．一方，(7e) のような文の文末イントネーションを上昇調にすると，丁寧な誘いの表現になります．

 (7f) は，時の副詞 already の意味からも推量の意味で使われていることが推測できます．

 習性・習慣の意味でよく知られる例は (7g, h) 以外にも，いたずらな男の子について述べた Boys will be boys.《諺》のような例で知られています．人にも物にも使われます．

### 1.2.2　shall の用法

 現代英語では，shall は (8) のように《英》で主に使われ，それ以外の (9) のような意味で使う場合は，will や be going to を使うのが普通になっています．

 一方，How *shall* I say it? (どう言えば良いかな) のようなフレーズがあります．また，(10a) のように時に *Shall* I ... / *Shall* we ... が提案の意味で使われますが，(10b) のようにくだけた会話では *Shall* I ...? の代わりに *Will* I ...? / *Will* we ...? が使われることがあります．

(8)　*Shall* I open the window?　《おもに英》[相手の意思を聞く]

(9)　a.　This time next week, I *shall* be in Scotland.　《英》[単純未来]

　　　b.　Candidates *shall* remain in their seats until all the papers have been collected.　《古風・文語》[命令]

　　　c.　I *shall* be leaving as soon as I am ready.　《堅い・まれ》[話者の意思]

(10)　a.　Let's try to use words that are in the dictionary next time, *shall* we?　《米》

　　　b.　A: *Will* I bring out the salads?　《米, くだけた》

　　　　　B: No. But, erm, is this fish cooked?

## 1.2.3　be going to の用法

　be going to は，実際の証拠や兆候がある場合の単純未来（予測）を言う (11a) のような場合と，実現の確実性が高い意思未来を言う (11b) のような場合に使われます．意思未来の意味の場合，will のようなその場で決めた意思ではなく，前もって決めている意思を表現します．

(11)　a.　It'*s going to* rain before evening; you'd better bring an umbrella with you.　　　　　　　　　　　　　　　　　　　　[単純未来]

　　　b.　He *is going to* be a dentist when he grows up.　　　　[意思未来]

## ＜もっと詳しく＞　☞『現代高等英文法』p. 126
「単純未来の will と going to の違い」

## 1.2.4　would の用法

(12)　a.　I thought he *would* be here sooner.　　　[will の過去；時制の一致]

　　　b.　They *would* reach the castle sometime.　　　[過去から見た未来]

　　　c.　I wish you *would* leave me alone.

　　　　　　　　　　　　　　　　　[wish の節で，実現可能性の低い願望]

　　　d.　If you went to see him, he'*d* be delighted.　[仮定法過去の帰結節で]

e.　Alex *would* never have found if you hadn't told him.

[仮定法過去完了の帰結節で]

f.　On Sundays he *would* get up early and go fishing in the sea.《文
語》　　　　　　　　　　　　　　　　　　[通例肯定形で，過去の習慣]

g.　I tried to persuade her, but she *would*n't allow me to come in.

[否定形で，苛立ち]

h.　I'*d* say he was about fifty.　　　　　　　　　　　　　[婉曲]

　(12a) では，時制の一致のために，伝達動詞 think の時制に合わせて will の過
去形の would が使われます．(12b) のように物語の作者が「後に…することにな
る」というように，過去から見た未来を意味する場合にも would が使われます．

　また，(12c) のように未来の実現が不可能であると思える事柄（仮想）を表現
する場合に wish が従える節において，さらに (12d, e) のように仮定法過去形・
仮定法過去完了形の帰結節において would が使われます．

　過去の習慣の意味を would で表す場合には，used to とは異なり，過去の習慣
の意味だと見てわかるような過去時の副詞や文脈が必要です．

　また，will と同様に，強い拒否にあった時の話者の強い苛立ちを表す (12g)
のような場合にも使われます．また，直接的な言い方を避けるために使われる I'*d*
like, I'*d* prefer, I'*d* hate, I'*d* think, I'*d* imagine, I'*d* say (＝(12h)) のような表
現でも使われます．

## ＜もっと詳しく＞　☞『現代高等英文法』p. 128
「過去の習慣の would と used to」

### 1.2.5　should の用法

　元々 shall の過去形である should ですが，shall が時制の一致のため過去形に
なる (13a) のような場合を除き，独自の意味を表します．(13b) のように「〜
するべきだ」という話し手の主張の意味を基本とし，(13c) のように推量や
(13d) のように指示の意味へと発展してきました．また，従属節の中で使うと
驚きの意味を表し，条件節の中で使うと堅苦しい言い方になります．遠回しに言

う時には，I should hope … / I should imagine … / I should hope so. / I should think so. / I should think not. などの表現があります．また，(13h) のように so that 節の中でも使われます．《文語》では，(13i) のように should が lest 節の中でも使われます．特に《米》では，should の代わりに直接法や仮定法現在が使われる傾向にあります．

(13) a.　I told him that I *should* be twenty next year.

　　　　　　　　　　　　　　　　　　　　[時制の一致；shall の過去形]

　　　b.　All people *should* have equal rights.　　　　　[話者の主張]

　　　c.　He *should* be in Chicago by now.　　　　　[推量・期待]

　　　d.　You *should* tell him straight what you think.　　　　[指示]

　　　e.　It is lucky that the weather *should* be so fine.　　　　[驚き]

　　　f.　If you *should* need anything else, do just let me know.

　　　　　　　　　　　　　　　　　　　　　[条件の if「もし仮に」]

　　　g.　He is a rude fellow, I *should* say.　　　[婉曲；主語は I, we に限る]

　　　h.　He wore a mask so that no one *should* recognize him.

　　　　　　　　　　　　　　　　　　　　　　[副詞節の so that 節で]

　　　i.　Lest anyone *should* doubt my story …

## ＜もっと詳しく＞　☞『現代高等英文法』p. 130
「lest 節内の should に代わる直接話法や仮定法現在」

### 1.2.6　can / could の用法

　can の基本的意味は永続的な能力です．現在時制と過去時制で使われ，一般的真理とされる用法も能力の意味から来ています．一方，「可能」の意味は，1 回ごとの行為について言う際に使います．知覚動詞の feel, hear, see, smell, taste などと共によく使います．

(14) a.　He *can* speak both English and French very well.　　[能力，現在]

　　　b.　I *could* drive before I left school.　　　　[能力，過去]

　　　c.　Steel *can* resist very high temperature.　　　　[一般的真理]

d. I *can* smell something burning. [可能，現在]

e. Luckily he *could* get to the hospital in time to witness the birth of his baby. [可能，過去]

## ＜もっと詳しく＞　☞『現代高等英文法』p. 134
「「能力」の意味の can と be able to / could が過去のことを言う場合」

相手に依頼をする表現 Can you …? / Could you …? は，後者がより丁寧な表現です（(15a, b)）。

「許可」の意味の can は，could で丁寧になります。また，会話では Can I …? / Could I …?（…してもいいですか）の形で使うことが多いです（(15c, d)）。

話者の判断による「可能性」の意味を表す can は，could が使用された時は話者の現在の判断を和らげた言い方になります（(15f)）。完了形では「過去の可能性」を表します（(15g)）。強い可能性について控えめに述べる際には，could well が使われます。また，could have + PP は，「…できたはずだ」という聞き手を非難する意味を表す場合があります（(15i)）。

(15j, k) は強い疑念を表す用法で，「まさかそんなことはないだろう」という意味合いがでます。

「能力」「許可」の場合に，伝達動詞の時制に合わせて時制の一致が起こり，過去形になります（(15l)）。

(15) a. *Can* you call back later? [依頼，現在]

b. *Could* you tell me how to go to the school? [依頼，過去，丁寧]

c. You *can* borrow five books at a time using your card. [許可，現在]

d. *Could* I interrupt a moment? [許可，現在，丁寧]

e. Speeding tickets *can* be over $500. [可能性，現在]

f. Motorists caught speeding *could* be fined £100. [可能性，現在]

g. I *could* have lost everything. [可能性，過去]

h. She *could* well be right, and she could be wrong.

[強い可能性，控えめ]

    i.   They *could* have let me know they were going to be late!

[過去, 非難]

    j.   *Can* he be the man who once ruled the society?

[疑問文で, 疑い・驚き]

    k.   *Could* he be the man who took Miss Gray to dinner?

[疑問文で, 疑い・驚き]

    l.   She said that she *could*n't come.    [時制の一致による can の過去形]

## 1.2.7　may/might の用法

　現在形の may は「可能性」「許可」「詠嘆的願望」の意味をもち, 過去形 might は現在のことを婉曲的に表現する場合にも使います.

　推量・可能性の意味の may は, may/might have + PP の形で「過去の出来事の不確実な推量」を表し, might have + PP で「実現しなかった過去の出来事の推量」を表すことがあります. might は, 実行されなかったことについて「…してもよさそうなものだ」の意味でも使われます. 他にも, 丁寧な提案の意味で You might ... が使われることがある点に注意が必要です. また, 時制の一致で might が使われることもあります.

　許可を求める表現 May I ...? にも使われ, この問いかけに対しては, 肯定の場合 "Of course (you can).", 否定の場合 "I'm sorry you can't." などと言います. より丁寧に許可を求めるのには might を使います. また, 古風な使い方として「詠嘆的願望」を表します.

　フレーズ扱いされる may/might well は, well が助動詞の意味を強め, 「可能性は十分ある」という話し手の推量を言います. また, may well (もっともだ) の意味は,「許可」の意味から来ていますが, 今では廃れていて (16l) のような一部のフレーズにのみ残っています.

　また, フレーズ may as well は《話》で「同じようなものだ」の意味で使われ, might as well はさらに表現を和らげるために使われます. had better とは同義ではありません.

  (16)　a.  He *may* be in London now.    [可能性, 現在のこと]

b. He *might* get there in time, but I can't be sure.

[可能性，現在のこと]

c. You *might* have said something that upset her.　[推量，過去のこと]

d. A lot of people died who *might* have been saved.

[推量，過去のこと，実現しなかったこと]

e. You *might* at least say thank you.　[現在のこと，実現しなかったこと]

f. They *might* have cleaned up before they left.

[過去のこと，実現しなかったこと]

g. Thirty minutes have passed.  If you have finished, you *may* leave. 《形式》　　　　　　　　　　　　　　　　　　　　　　[許可]

h. *Might* I borrow your pen?　　　　　　　　　　[許可，丁寧]

i. *May* God grant you happiness.《古》　　　　　　[詠嘆的願望]

j. We are going to a concert.  You *might* like to come with us.

[丁寧な提案]

k. I bought him some sandwiches because I thought he *might* be hungry.　　　　　　　　　　　　　　　　　　[時制の一致]

l. What you say *may* very well be true.

[推量，may（可能性がある）を well（十分に）が強める]

m. "What do they hope to achieve?" "You *might* well ask."

[フレーズ，「答えるのは難しい」の意味]

n. We *may* as well start the meeting——the others will be here soon.

[フレーズ]

o. They *might* as well have a badge on them saying "Steal me."

[フレーズ]

## 1.2.8　must の用法

「義務・命令」「推断」の意味で使われる must は，過去形がないので過去のことは had to で，また，未来のことは will have to/shall have to で表します。

　義務の意味の must は，（17d）では話し手から文の主語である聞き手に与える義務を表し，（17e）では I must ... で話し手が自分自身に対して与える義務を表

します．聞き手に話し手の義務があるかどうか尋ねる Must I …? に対する答え方は，(17f) のようになります．ここでは，must の否定文は，禁止の意味になりちぐはぐな受け答えになるので don't have to を使います．また，話し手・聞き手が課す義務は must を，法律などの決まりごとについては have to を使うという違いがあります．

(17h) の否定文では，禁止の意味になります．(17i) は，相手に指示を与えるので親しい人への強い勧誘の意味にもなります．

(18a, b) のように推断の意味（〜にちがいない）で使われますが，《米》では推断の意味を表すのに have to/have got to がよく使われます．過去の推断は must have + PP（〜だったにちがいない）で表しますが，have to have + PP で表すこともあります．また，推断の否定は can't（「はずがない」）を使います．

(17) a.　I missed my connecting flight and *had to* stay in Paris overnight.

　　　　　　　　　　　　　　　　　　　　　　　　　　　　　　　[過去]

　　 b.　We will *have to* wait a few more weeks.　　　　　[未来]

　　 c.　I shall *have to* think more on it.　　　　　　　　[未来]

　　 d.　You *must* be here before eight o'clock tomorrow.　[義務・命令]

　　 e.　I *must* go now, or I'll be late.　　　　　　　　　[義務]

　　 f.　*Must* I finish it tonight? — Yes, you *must.* / No, you don't *have to.*

　　 g.　You *have to* drive on the left in Britain.　[義務，法的な決まりごと]

　　 h.　Cars *must* not be parked in front of the entrance.　[否定文で，禁止]

　　 i.　You *must* come and see me from time to time.　[勧誘；《主に英》]

(18) a.　Judging from the way he talks, he *must* be Japanese.　[推断]

　　 b.　I think the book *must* have been written in the 80s or 90s.

　　　　　　　　　　　　　　　　　　　　　　　　　　　　[推断，過去]

　　 c.　Somebody *has to* have seen her.

　　 d.　He *can't* be Japanese.

　　　　　　　[推断の否定，《米》で He must not be Japanese. とも言う]

## 1.3　準法助動詞

### 1.3.1　have to / have got to / had to の用法

「義務」の意味で，話し手の意思を言う must とは異なり，have（got）to は一般的な義務や要請を言います．

否定形（don't have to / haven't got to）は，「…する必要がない」の意味になります．イギリス英語では have not to の形もありますが，その使用はまれです．don't have to have＋PP は，「…し終わっている必要はない」の意味になります．

(19b) のように，must と同じく，相手に義務を課して強く勧める表現法もあります．(20), (21) は，義務の否定を示しています．「推断」の用法は，(22), (23) のような表現でよく使われます．

(19) a.　You *have to* sign your name here.　　　　　　　　　［義務］

　　　b.　You *have to* come and meet my wife some time.　　　［強い勧誘］

(20)　You don't *have to* go to school every day, do you?

　　　＝You *have*n't *got to* go to school every day, have you?

(21)　You don't *have to* have read a book to have an opinion on it.　［義務］

(22)　There *has*（*got*）*to* be some reason for his absurd behavior.　《主に米》

　　　　　　　　　　　　　　　　　　　　　　　　　　　　　　　［推断］

(23) a.　You *have*（*got*）*to* be joking / kidding.　　　　　　　　［推断］

　　　b.　Someone *has to* lose the game.　　　　　　　　　　　　［推断］

### 1.3.2　be to の用法

準法助動詞の be to の be は，現在形と過去形のみで使われます．「…することになっている」という確定した予定の意味が基本（＝(24a)）で，聞き手に対して使うと (24b) のように命令になり，聞き手全員に対して使うと (24c) のように規則の意味になります．(24d) は運命とも言われる用法で，過去形で使われ，史実を知っている人が過去の時点から未来を予測する意味で使われています（would の［過去から見た未来］の用法と同じ）．準助動詞の be to は，(25) のような「be 動詞＋to 不定詞」の表現とは異なるため混同しないように注意が必

要です．一方，(26a) のように条件節の am / are / is to は願望を，(26b) のよう
な条件節の were to は実現しそうにない現在の仮定を言うのに使われます．

(24) a.　The Prime Minister *is to* speak on television tonight. [確定した予定]

　　 b.　You *are to* be here by six tomorrow morning.　　　　　 [命令]

　　 c.　All prisoners *are to* be in bed by 10 o'clock.　　　　 [規則]

　　 d.　Caesar returned to Italy and proclaimed himself the permanent
　　　　 "dictator" of Rome.  He *was to* pay dearly for his ambition in due
　　　　 course.　　　　　　　　　　　　　　　　 [過去から見た未来]

(25) a.　He *is to* blame.　　　　　　　　　　 [be 動詞＋to 不定詞]

　　 b.　This letter *is to* tell you that you've done a good job.

　　　　　　　　　　　　　　　　　　　 [to 不定詞の名詞用法]

　　 c.　The porter *was* nowhere *to* be found.　 [to 不定詞の副詞用法]

(26) a.　If we *are to* win the competition, we must start training now.

　　　　　　　　　　　　　　　　　　 [条件節の am / are / is to]

　　 b.　If you *were to* learn Spanish, you might get a better job.

　　　　　　　　　　　　　　　　　　　　 [条件節の were to]

## 1.3.3　be about to の用法

be about to は「まさに…しようとする」の意味になり，否定文は「起こりそ
うにない」の意味になります．ただ，一人称主語の場合，否定文は「…したくな
い」の意味になる点に注意が必要です．

(27) a.　We arrived just as the ceremony *was about to* begin.

　　 b.　Well, that'*s* not *about to* happen or is it?

　　 c.　I've never done any cooking and I'*m* not *about to* start now.

　　　　　　　　　　　　　　　　　　　　 [一人称主語，否定で]

## 1.3.4　ought to の用法

ought to は must に似て「義務」と「推断」の意味をもちます．義務の場合，
完了形を従えると，果たされなかった義務の意味になります．否定形は ought

not to, 《米》では時に oughtn't to が使われます．(28c) の疑問文は《まれ》ですが，(28d) のように Do you think … ought to …? で言い換えて表現できます．「義務」の意味においても「推断」の意味においても，ought to は must より控えめな意味になります．

(28) a.　You *ought to* be more careful of your health.　　　　[義務]

　　 b.　You *ought to* have apologized.

　　　　　　　　　　　　　　　　[完了形をとって，はたされなかった義務]

　　 c.　*Ought* I *to* write to say thank you?　《まれ》　　　[疑問文で，義務]

　　 d.　*Do you think* I *ought to* write to say thank you?

　　　　　　　　　　　　　　　　　　　[疑問文，(c) の言い換え]

　　 e.　If he started at nine, he *ought to* be here by now.　　[推断]

### 1.3.5　need の用法

　法助動詞 need は「必要だ」の意味を表しますが，動詞用法で同じ意味を表現できるので，法助動詞の使用頻度は低く，主に疑問文・否定文で用いられます．否定文・疑問文の作り方は，他の法助動詞に準じます．一方，「…が必要である」の意味の動詞 need は need to の形をとり，肯定文，疑問文，否定文で使われます．

　また，過去を表す場合，法助動詞の (needn't have + PP) は「その必要がなかった」の意味を表し，動詞の didn't need to は「必要がなかったからしなかった」の意味を表すという違いがあります．

(29) a.　You *needn't* come to the office on Saturday.

　　　　　　　　　　　　　　　　[法助動詞の否定文；義務の免除]

　　　　cf. You *don't need to* come home every weekend.　　[動詞の否定文]

　　 b.　*Need* I pay the whole amount now?　　[法助動詞の疑問文；必要]

　　　　cf. *Do* I *need to* pay for this now?　　　　　　[動詞の疑問文]

　　 c.　You *needn't have* woken me up. I don't have to go to work today.

　　 d.　It started raining, so I *didn't need to* water the flowers.

## 1.3.6   dare の用法

「あえて…する」の意味を表す法助動詞 dare は，動詞用法で同じ意味を表現できるので，法助動詞としての使用頻度は低く，主に《英》で疑問文・否定文で用いられます．否定文・疑問文の作り方は他の法助動詞と同じです．ただ，否定文の場合，(30b, c) のように don't を伴う動詞としての性質と，原形を伴う法助動詞の性質をもった混交形が使われます．この混交形は "Don't you dare …!" という強迫的な表現になってよく用いられます．

(30) a.  How *dare* you speak to me so rudely?          [法助動詞の疑問文：勇気]

　　　　cf. John *dared to* defy the theory taken for granted for more than

　　　　　　one hundred years.                                       [動詞]

　　b.  I'm tired.  I haven't slept in a month.  I *don't dare* close my eyes?

　　　　　　　　　　　　　　　　　　　　　　　　　　　　　[混交文]

　　c.  Yes, *don't* you *dare* come over smoking!          [混交形，強迫]


## 1.3.7   had better/had best の用法

had better は主語に対する強い指示や勧告，脅迫を言うのに使います．否定文の not の位置（had better not …）や疑問文（Had I …），否定疑問文（Hadn't I …?）の作り方に注意が必要です．時に had best になったり，くだけた会話では had を省いて better だけになることもあります．主語に対する強い指示や勧告を伝える表現ですが，I が主語になって話し手の決心を表します．

(31) a.  You'*d better* go and see your teacher right away.          [強い指示]

　　b.  You'*d better* not see the movie.                        [強い勧告]

　　c.  "I'll give back the money tomorrow."  "You'*d better*!"          [脅迫]

　　d.  *Had* I *better* see the movie?

　　e.  *Had*n't we *better* tell him the truth?

　　f.  You *had best* put down the weapon, Mr. Johnson.

　　g.  When he is in the room, you *better* know what you are talking

　　　　about.

## ＜もっと詳しく＞　☞『現代高等英文法』p. 146
「had better の主語」

### 1.3.8　used to の用法

used to は，今はない過去の状態・行動について述べる時に使われます．疑問形・否定形は Did he use to …?/He didn't use to … となります．否定文の He used not to … は《古風》で，He usen't to … が《英》で用いられることもあります．Used he to …? とする疑問文は《非標準》です．

(32) a.　I always *used to* be afraid of dogs.　　　　　　[過去の継続的状態]

　　 b.　A: She is very tall, isn't she?

　　　　 B: Yes, she *used to* do ballet.　　　　　　　　[過去の行動]

　　 c.　Where *did* you *use to* live before you moved here?

　　　　　　　　　　　　　　　　　　　　　　　[疑問文，-d を省く]

　　 d.　I *didn't use to* like him, but now we're good friends.

　　　　　　　　　　　　　　　　　　　　　　　[否定文，-d を省く]

## 2　助動詞が完了形を従える場合の意味

法助動詞の中には，意味によって「完了形（have＋PP）」を従えるものがあります．実際に起こったこと（実現した行為），あるいは起こるであろうこと（実現したと思われる行為）を言う場合と，実際には起こらなかったことを言う場合があります．ただし，be going to, be to, dare, used to, be about to は完了をとることはなく，ought to は意味によって両方の使い方があります．

### 2.1　実現した（と思われる）行為

行為の予測を言う法助動詞（will, shall, may, might, must, have to, ought to, need, had better）は，すでに起こったこと，あるいは，起こるであろうことに

ついての話し手の判断を表します.

(33) a. He *will have finished* his dinner by the time we arrive.　[未来完了]

　　 b. I *shall have been staying* there for five months by that time.　《英》

　　　　　　　　　　　　　　　　　　　　　　　　　　　　　　[未来完了]

　　 c. John *may have left* already.　　　　　　　　　　　　　　[推量]

　　 d. Since the ditch is full of water, it *must have rained* last night.

　　　　　　　　　　　　　　　　　　　　　　　　　　　　　　[推断]

(34) a. Every week we *have to have finished* reading a whole novel and a

　　　　small quiz is given the next class date.　　　　　　　　　[義務]

　　 b. She had been a nurse for over 40 years; she *had to have known*

　　　　she was dying.　　　　　　　　　　　　　　　　　　　　[推断]

(35) a. He *ought to have arrived* there by now, if he had caught the 3:30

　　　　train.　　　　　　　　　　　　　　　　　　　　　　　　[推断]

　　 b. You *needn't have come* if you had been so busy.　　　　　[必要]

　　 c. If you are giving your readers advice, then you'*d better have tried*

　　　　it out yourself first.　　　　　　　　　　　　　　　　　[勧告]


## 2.2  未実現の行為

　仮定の帰結を言う法助動詞 (would, could, should, might, ought to) は, 実現
されなかったことについての話し手の見解を述べます. 次の例には, それぞれ
(　) に示すような事実が背景にあります.

(36) a. If you had taken a taxi, you *would have got* there in time.

　　　　(You didn't get there in time.)

　　 b. How I wished I *could have been* with him!

　　　　(I couldn't be with him.)

　　 c. You *should have studied* more.

　　　　(You didn't study so much.)

　　 d. You *might have been killed* if you had been with them.

（You weren't killed because you weren't with them.）

e.　They *ought to have made* for the back door.

　　（They didn't make for the back door.）


# ◉練習問題◉

**1　次の空所（　　）に入る語を選択肢から選びなさい.**

1.1　You will （　　　　　） to understand English if you study with this book.

1.2　TAXI DRIVER: "Where do you want to go, sir?"

　　　PASSENGER: "I （　　　　） to go to the nearest station."

1.3　"Would you like some tea or coffee?  Or would you like some green tea?"

　　　"I'd （　　　） have a Scotch and water, please."

1.4　Be （　　　） to be here by eight tomorrow.  We will leave by eight ten.

1.5　I don't （　　　） ask you why you didn't do the homework.

　選択肢：come, dare, would, like, rather, sure


**2　次の英文を日本語訳しなさい.**

2.1　The central concourse of Osaka Station was so crowded that I couldn't find the person I had arranged to meet.

2.2　Why don't we stay at the Prince Hotel when we go to Tokyo?

2.3　"Can I go to the restroom?"  "You should have gone before the class started."

2.4　If you major in economics, you should at least read a newspaper everyday and follow what's happening in the world.

2.5　I can't forgive you for what you said.

_____

## 3　（　　）の中の語句を使用して，以下の日本語を英語にしなさい.

3.1　高田さん，すみませんが，ちょっとお時間ありますか. (could / spare)

_____

3.2　今晩おじゃまするよ. (call on)

_____

3.3　奈良ではあまり雪は降らない. (We [or They])

_____

3.4　そろそろ昼ご飯を食べに行こうか. (now)

_____

3.5　前期の試験は良くなかったので，後期は一生懸命やります.
　　　(the first / second semester, do well)

_____

# 第4章　法と仮定法構文

（『現代高等英文法』pp. 150 ～ 166 に該当）

## 1　法と仮定法構文

### 1.1　法とは

　法（mood）とは，「話し手の気持ち」の意味です．英語では①〜④の方法で，それを表現することができます．

① 動詞の変化形（例：一人称の were など）や構文（例：If I were a bird, ….)

② 法助動詞（will, shall, can, may, must など）

③ "It is that," "It seems that," "It is a pity that," "It is dreadful that" のような構文

④ 副詞（離接詞：例：fortunately（幸運にも））

本章は，①に焦点を当てて見ていきます．動詞の形を変化させた法は，Table 2.4.1 のようなものがあります．

Table 2.4.1　法の表現方法

| 法の種類 | 動詞の形 |
|---|---|
| 直説法（indicative mood） | 時制・数・相に応じて変化する定形 |
| 仮定法（subjunctive mood） | 法助動詞の過去形，動詞の原形，過去形，完了形 |
| 命令法（imperative mood） | 動詞の原形 |

## 1.2  直説法・命令法と仮定法構文

直説法は，（1a）のような例が最も一般的な形です．命令法は，動詞の原形を使う文で，PART I 第 2 章 4 で解説しました．

仮定法には，Table 2.4.2 のようなものがあります．

Table 2.4.2　仮定法の種類とそれらの特徴

| 仮定法構文の種類 | 意味的特徴 | 動詞の形 | 用例 |
|---|---|---|---|
| 仮定法現在形 | 忠告・命令・指示など | 原形 | (1b) |
| 仮定法過去形 | 現在の事実に反すること | 過去形 | (1c) |
| 仮定法過去完了形 | 過去の事実に反すること | 過去完了形 | (1d) |
| 願望仮定法 | 願望（古い英語の名残） | 原形 | (1e) |

(1)  a.  I *was* sick, so I *didn't* go to school yesterday.          [直説法]

　　 b.  It is requested that you *be* present at the meeting tomorrow.

　　 c.  If I *were* you I would give up.

　　 d.  If I *had* not *been* sick, I would have gone to school yesterday.

　　 e.  Manners *be* hanged! / God *bless* the Queen! / Heaven *forbid*.


## 2　仮定法現在形構文

仮定法現在形構文（subjunctive present construction）では，（2）のように要請，勧告，意思，指示など（以下，まとめて「指示」と言う）の意味の動詞が使われる主節に続く従属節で，動詞の原形（仮定法現在形と言う．イタリック表示）が使われることがあります．

(2)  a.  The class insists that you *be* the spokesman.

　　 b.  I recommend that he *see* a doctor.

　　 c.  The committee has asked that this scheme *be* stopped for now.

仮定法現在形を導く動詞には，下記のようなものがあります．

advise, agree, allow, arrange, ask, beg, command, concede, decide, decree, demand, desire, determine, enjoin, ensure, entreat, grant, insist, instruct, intend, move, ordain, order, pledge, pray, prefer, pronounce, propose, recommend, request, resolve, rule, stipulate, suggest, urge, vote など

また (3), (4) のように，特定の形容詞や名詞が使われる主節に続く従属節で仮定法現在形 (イタリック表示) が使われることもあります．

(3) a.　It is important that he *attend* every day.
    b.　It is essential that our pilots *be* given the best possible training.
(4) a.　It was his wish that she *have* it.
    b.　It was his idea that I *join* the club.

仮定法現在を導く形容詞及び名詞は，下記の通りです．

形容詞：advisable, apparent, certain, compulsory, critical, crucial, essential, fitting, imperative, important, impossible, indispensable, mandatory, necessary, obligatory, paramount, proper, unnecessary, urgent, vital など
名詞：claim, decision, idea, insistence, intention, suggestion, wish など

　仮定法現在形構文で使われる接続詞に，(5) の lest と whether があります．特に，whether は whether it be ... やフレーズ化した表現 whether these be / whether they be などで使われます．これらに後続する節の中では，動詞の原形のほかに (5b) のように should が使われることもあります．

(5) a.　He was concerned **lest** anyone *think* that he was guilty.
    b.　It is in fact open to question **whether** it *should* be allowed at all.
    c.　The first five pages reveals the necessary elements of good writing, **whether** it *be* fiction, nonfiction, journalism, or poetry.

# 3　条件と直説法・仮定法過去形・仮定法過去完了形

## 3.1　条件と仮定

　「もし…だったら」という条件は，ifで表されます．そのifで表される条件には，「もし氷を加熱したら」というような想定の場合と，高齢者が「もし若かったら」というような仮定の場合があります．普通は，仮定は仮定法過去形，あるいは仮定法過去完了で表現します．(6) は，因果関係を想定して，直説法で表現した例です．

(6) a.　If you heat ice, it melts.　　　　　　　　[因果関係，直説法現在]

　　b.　If you add 4 to 5, you get 9.　　　　　　[因果関係，直説法現在]

## 3.2　開放条件

　条件には，開放条件と却下条件があります．「開放条件」(open condition) は，(7a, b) のように予測通りの事態が生じるかどうか不明ですが，「もしそうなれば」という条件を述べるものです．開放条件では，事態が生じる可能性が低い場合に (7c) のように should が使われることがあります．if を使わずに主語と should の倒置によって，開放条件を表現する (7d) のような場合もあります．will が，未来でなく意思，丁寧などを表す場合は，開放条件の if 節の中で使われることがあります．

(7) a.　We can manage **if you *let* us know in time**. [開放条件，直説法現在]

　　b.　**If it *is* clear tomorrow**, we'll go hiking.　　[開放条件，直説法現在]

　　c.　**If we *should* miss the 10 o'clock train**, we shan't get there till after lunch.

　　d.　***Should* you lose one of your credit cards**, call your emergency helpline.

　　e.　**If you *will* reserve seats**, we shall be sure of a comfortable journey.

## 3.3　却下条件

「却下条件」（rejected condition）は，事実に反する仮定をする場合です．(8)
を見てください．通常，却下条件では仮定法が用いられます．(8a) は現在の仮
想であり，動詞・法助動詞の過去形を使います．(8b) は過去の出来事が起こっ
ていなければ，という過去の仮想であり，動詞の過去完了形・法助動詞の過去形
＋have＋PP が使われます．

　却下条件が wish などの動詞，主語または to 不定詞で表されることもありま
す．

<br>

(8) a.　**If I** *were* **an American**, I wouldn't have any difficulty learning
　　　English.　　　　　　　　　　　　　　　　[却下条件，仮定法過去]

　　b.　**If I** *had seen* **you walking**, I could have offered you a lift.

　　　　　　　　　　　　　　　　　　　　[却下条件，仮定法過去完了]

<br>

## 3.4　条件の表し方

　条件は if や主語と操作詞（should, had, were など）の倒置によるほか，if 以
外の接続詞で表現されることがあります．現代英語では開放条件を導く (9) の
unless などと，開放条件も却下条件も導く (10) の suppose などに分けられま
す．仮定法過去完了形の代わりをする (11) の but for（もし…がなければ）のよう
な語句もあります．

<br>

(9)　I can't help you **unless you** *tell* **me what's wrong**.　　[開放条件]

(10) a.　**Suppose we** *miss* **the train**—what will we do then?　　[開放条件]

　　b.　**Suppose you** *won* **the lottery**, what would you do with the mon-
　　　ey?　　　　　　　　　　　　　　　　　　　　[却下条件]

(11)　**But for Jenny**, we would have lost the match.

　　　（＝If Jenny hadn't played, ….）

<br>

開放条件を導く表現：as long as, once, on condition that; assuming, given that,
　　　　　　　　　granted, provided, say, unless

開放条件と却下条件を導く表現：suppose, supposing, as if, as though, but for, like（口語）

## 4  仮定法過去形構文

### 4.1  if 節による条件の表し方

　仮定法過去形構文は，動詞や一部の法助動詞の過去形を使って，現在の仮想を表現します．仮定法過去形構文の基本型は，(12) のような「if＋主語＋動詞/法助動詞の過去形 ...，主語＋would/could など＋原形動詞」ですが，if 節は主節の前に来ることも後に来ることもあります．

(12) a.  *If* I *had* lots of money, I *would* give some to anybody who asked for it.
　　 b.  *If* she *were* to try harder next time, she *would* pass the exam.
　　 c.  If you *could* type, you *might* save a lot of time.

### 4.2  if 節以外の条件の表し方

　(13) の例を見てください．if 節以外の条件の表し方は (13) のように，倒置もしくは wish などの動詞で表現されます．

　(14) は，it is (high) time/it is (about) time＋仮定法となっている例です．仮定法過去形が来るのがもっとも標準的ですが，現在形，原形，should なども来ます．ただし，be 動詞は I was/she was/he was のように was が普通で were はまれです．

　(15) のように仮定法過去形を導くフレーズもあります．(15c) も仮定法過去形の were を含んだフレーズで，それと同じ意味で使われる but for のような語句もあります．その帰結節には would, could が使われます．

　(16a) の "it would be a good idea if ..." は相手に対する忠告の意味のフレー

ズで，if 節には仮定法過去形が来ます．(16b) は一部の叙述形容詞がとる型で使われる仮定法過去形です．

(13) a. *Were* she in charge, she *would* do things differently. 《文語》

[語順倒置]

    b. I wish I *were* rich.

    c. I wish you *could* come with me.

(14) It's time I *was* going. ( = 《英》 It's time I should be going.)

(15) a. If only I *were* not so nervous. (もっと平静でいられたらいいのだが)

    b. I'd rather you *were* in bed. (もう寝ていて欲しいな)

    c. If it *were not for* ( = But for) the rescue team I wouldn't be alive today.

(16) a. I think it *would* be a good idea if you *left* before I inform the authorities.

    ["it's a good idea to do" という婉曲的な忠告の意味のフレーズを would を使ってより婉曲にした表現]

    b. It *would* be helpful if you *stayed*.

## 4.3　条件が明示されない場合

仮定法構文は条件がなければ成り立ちませんが，条件が明示されず，表面的に帰結節だけの場合があります．主語が仮定の条件となる I wouldn't do that. や to 不定詞が条件になっている You'd be surprised to see him. のような例が挙げられます．

# 5　仮定法過去完了形構文

仮定法過去完了形構文は，過去完了形を用いて過去の事実に反する仮定を表し，帰結節でその仮定の結果を述べます．これは，(17) のような「if + 主語 +

had + PP / 法助動詞の過去形 + have + PP, 主語 + would / could など + have + PP」
の形で表されます. (18) も仮定法過去完了形を使用した例です.

(17) a. If you *had done* as I told you, you *would have succeeded.*

　　 b. If they *hadn't told* us, we *wouldn't have found* the way.

　　 c. I *might have married* her if she *would have agreed.*

(18) a. He looked as if he *had seen* a ghost.

　　 b. I wish I *hadn't told* them.

　　 c. Adam *would have faced* almost certain death, if it *hadn't been for*
　　　　 his quick thinking.

　　 d. *Had* he *known* the truth, he *would have gotten* mad.　（文語）


# 6　仮定法構文の異形

　仮定法構文で, 条件と帰結を表現する方法は, 仮定法過去形 (「if + 主語 + 動
詞 / 法助動詞の過去形 ..., 主語 + would / could など + 原形動詞」) や仮定法過去
完了形 (「if + 主語 + had + PP / 法助動詞 + have + PP ..., 主語 + would / could な
ど + have + PP」) に限りません. 異形や混合形について (19) を見てみましょう.

　(19a) は仮定法過去形構文の異形の例で, if 節で却下条件を表していますが,
「(もし…だったとしても) そんなことはどうでも良い」という表現です.

(19) a. *I don't care* if they were Martians.

　　 b. *It didn't matter* if they were Republican or Democrat.

　　 c. *What* if they weren't dead?

　2つ目は, 仮定法過去形と仮定法過去完了形の混合形です. 却下条件には, ①
「もし今 A なら B なのに」(仮定法過去形), ②「もしあの時 A だったら B だっ
ただろうに」(仮定法過去完了形) という 2 つのタイプ以外に, ③ (20) の「もし
あの時 A だったら, 今は B だろうに」も, ④ (21) の「もし今 A なら, あの時
B だっただろう」のタイプもあります.

(20) a. If he *had known* just enough, he'*d* be alive today.

[過去の仮定＋現在の状態]

b. If he *had come*, then there *would* be no problem.

[過去の仮定＋現在の状態]

(21) a. If I *were* a US citizen, I *would have voted* for him.

[現在の仮定＋過去の結果]

b. If he *were* really working to help this country, he *would have given* up on his impossible bid for the presidency and …

[現在の仮定＋過去の結果]

3つ目は，仮定法過去完了形の異形です．時に，仮定法過去完了形を仮定法過去形で代用する場合があります．

(22) a. If I *knew* you were coming, I'*d have baked* a cake.

[本来 If I had known … の形]

b. If I *had* the money with me, I *would have bought* you one.

[本来 If I had had … の形]

## 7 願望仮定法

次の (23) は現代英語に残っている願望仮定法で，すべて文語です．(23) の例は，フレーズのように使用されるため，それらの構造の説明は難しいです．(23a) 以外は，主語と仮定法現在形の語順が入れ替わっていることが特徴的です．

(23) a. Heaven *forbid* that war should break out.

b. *Be* it ever so humble, there's no place like home.

c. *Come* hunting season, a rifle replaces the rod.

d. *Suffice* it to say that we won.

e. *Be* that as it may, we have nothing to lose.

 f. You can teach him if need *be*.

 g. If you've really decided to quit the music business, then so *be* it.


# ◉練習問題◉

## 1　以下の英文を日本語訳しなさい.

1.1 If my car had not broken, I could have caught the train.

_____

1.2 If it is convenient, let's meet at nine o'clock.

_____

1.3 If he were my child, I'd be proud of him.

_____

1.4 How I wish I could speak English fluently!

_____

1.5 "Tell me the way to the post office."

  "Go straight along this road and turn right at the second corner, and you'll see it."

_____


## 2　次の（　　）内の語句を並び替えて, 意味の通る適切な英文にしなさい.

2.1 I (if / how to do / show / knew myself / would / it / you / I).

_____

2.2 The child would (hadn't stopped / killed / the train / have / been / if / quickly).

_____

2.3 If you (get / be able to / can / type, / ought to / a job / you).

_____

2.4 If you don't (don't / have time / we / why / this evening, / make a date) tomorrow.

_____

2.5 If you (a student driver / cause / while / an accident / you / are), your temporary license (be / revoked / will).

_____

## 3 （　　）内の語句を使って，次の日本語を英語にしなさい．

3.1 もし知っていたら私，行っただろうにな．(would / known)

_____

3.2 夕飯がまだ準備できてなければ，ご飯抜きで行くつもりです．

_____

3.3 その犬を繋いでなければ，君を噛んでいただろうな．(would / be tied up)

_____

3.4 明日の英語の授業が休講だったらな．

_____

3.5 運転免許がとれたらどこへ行きたいですか．

_____

# 第5章 話法と時制の一致

（『現代高等英文法』pp. 182 〜 192 に該当）

## 1 話法とは

### 1.1 話法の種類

　話法 (speech) とは，話し手の言葉を聞き手が第三者に伝える方法のことです．人が実際に話した言葉を引用して伝える (1a) を「直接話法」(direct speech)，話し手の言葉に言い換えて伝える (1b) を「間接話法」(indirect speech) と言います．

　話法の種類に関係なく，主動詞を「伝達動詞」(reporting verb) と言い，伝達する内容の部分を「被伝達部」(reported part)，そして被伝達部を導入する部分（つまり主節）を「伝達部」(reporting part) と言います．伝達動詞には，「話す」「考える」「伝える」のような意味の say, tell, report, think, announce, ask, order などがあります．

  (1) a.  He said to me, "I visited Ise Shrine on New Year's Day."

[直接話法]

      b.  He told me that he had visited Ise Shrine on New Year's Day.

[間接話法]

### 1.2 話法の転換

　話法の転換とは，同じ内容を話法を変えて表現することで，転換する場合に

は, 時制・人称・時の副詞などを修正します. 例えば, (1b) は (1a) と違って, 引用符がない, 引用符の前のカンマがない, また, 動詞・代名詞が言い換えられています. (2a) と (2b) のような例を比較しながら見てみると, 話法の転換に伴う修正は, 話法の転換というより, 同じ内容を別の方法で表現すると言った方が正確でしょう.

(2) a. "Why don't we go to Kobe, Yoshiko?" said Jiro. [直接話法]
    b. Jiro suggested to Yoshiko going to Kobe. [間接話法]

## 1.3 中間話法

小説などでは,「中間話法」(middle speech) あるいは「描出話法」(represented speech) といわれる話法が使われることがあります. (3) のように, 引用符がなく (間接話法的), 時制・人称・時の副詞・語順などの一部あるいは全部が実際に話された言葉の引用あるいはそれに近いもの (直接話法的) なので, 直接話法と間接話法の中間的な表現方法です.

(3) The screen showed a map. It appeared to be some woods and a river. *That must be where I am*, he thought. Feeling a little braver, he pressed the button under the middle screen which lit up to show a lot of lines and colored stripes and bars. *Wonder what they all do?*, he thought. (Trevor Meredith, *Isaiah's Exceptional Day* (2006))

[中間話法]

## ＜もっと詳しく＞ ☞『現代高等英文法』p. 184
「なぜ直接話法は say, 間接話法は tell か」

## 1.4 伝達動詞のリスト

伝達動詞は意思伝達を行う動詞のことで, 次のようなものを指します. ただし, これらの動詞は必ずしも直接・間接話法の両方の話法をとるとは限りませ

ん.

伝達動詞の一例 : add, admit, advise, agree, answer, argue, ask, beg, believe, claim, comment, complain, conclude, confirm, consider, continue, cry, decide, demand, doubt, expect, explain, feel, hear, imagine, inform, insist, instruct, know, learn, mention, observe, offer, order, predict, promise, propose, read, recommend, refuse, remark, repeat, reply, report, request, say, scream, shout, state, suggest, suppose, swear, tell, thank, think, understand, warn, whisper, wonder, write など

(4) のような動作や表情などでも意思伝達は可能です. また, talk と speak は伝達動詞ではなく, 直接・間接話法の伝達部にはなれません.

> (4) a. I *nodded* that I was aware of these types.
> b. "Yes," I *smiled*.

## 1.5　直接話法の伝達部の語順

直接話法の伝達部は, (5) のように引用の後に来ると主語と動詞が倒置を起こすことがありますが, 主語が代名詞の場合には, 倒置は起こりません.

> (5) a. "Nice to see you," Phil said／said Phil.
> b. "Nice to see you," he said.

## 1.6　人称代名詞・時・場所の副詞の転換

話法が変わると人称代名詞・時の副詞を転換する必要が生じることが多いですが, 機械的に書き換えるのではありません. 文脈や状況によってもとのままの場合もあります. 転換の際に用いる代表的な語と, その語と対応関係にある語を覚えておくとよいでしょう.

Table 2.5.1　話法による転換

| 人称代名詞 | He said to me, "You ..." | → | He told me that I ... |
|---|---|---|---|
| | She said to me, "I ..." | → | She told me that she ... |
| 時 | now | → | then, at that time |
| | today | → | that day |
| | yesterday | → | the day before |
| | tomorrow | → | the next day |
| | this week | → | that week |
| | last year | → | the year before |
| | next month | → | the following month |
| | an hour ago | → | an hour before |
| 場所 | here | → | there, at that place |
| | there | → | there |

## 2　文の種類による直接話法と間接話法の対応関係

　ここでは直接話法を間接話法に変えた場合，どのような変化を起こすのか，時制，伝達動詞，人称代名詞，副詞（これらを直示（deictic）要素と言います）を中心に見ていきます．

### 2.1　命令文→間接命令文

　命令文の原形動詞は，to 不定詞になります．人称代名詞の you が誰であるかわかればその人を表すのにふさわしい名詞・代名詞に代えます．

(6) a.　"Go away." → He told me to go away.

　　b.　"Wash your face." → My mother told me to wash my face.

　　c.　"Fold it in half." → She asked me to fold it in half.

　　d.　"Come in." → The policeman ordered the suspect to come in.

## 2.2　平叙文→間接平叙文

平叙文から間接平叙文への書き換えは，(7) のようになります．伝達動詞 admit は，直説話法では被伝達部の後に多く来ますが，間接話法では被伝達部の前に来る必要があります．

(7) a.　Jill said to me, "They *don't* know you."

→ Jill told me that they *didn't* know me.

[伝達動詞の過去形に合わせて過去形]

b.　Father said, "There *was* a fire near the bus stop."

→ Father said that there *was* a fire near the bus stop.

[事故の報告は過去形]

c.　The teacher said to us, "You *are* not working hard enough."

→ The teacher told us that we *were* not working hard enough.

d.　Mother said to me, "You *must* go at once."

→ Mother told me that I *had to* go at once.

[must は過去形がないから had to]

e.　"This *will* be the first time that I've given evidence in a trial," he admitted.

→ He admitted that this *would* be the first time he'd given evidence in a trial.

## 2.3　疑問文→間接疑問文

疑問文を間接疑問文にすると平叙文の語順になります．

(8) a.　"How did you do that?"

→ They wanted to know how I had done it.

b.　"Why does he sing so loudly?"

→ We wonder why he sings so loudly.

c.　"Are these shoes of yours of Italian make?"

　　　　→ The clerk asked me if those shoes of mine were of Italian make.

　d.　"Shall I hurry on and get the tickets?"

　　　　→ He asked if he should hurry on and get the tickets.

## 2.4　感嘆文→間接感嘆文

　how, what を使った感嘆文は，前置詞の目的語になる場合はそのまま間接感嘆文にします．それ以外は，感嘆の内容によって動詞を選択したり，how の代わりに very で意味を強めるなどの書き換えが必要です．

　(9)　a.　"How fast he runs!"

　　　　→ I was surprised how fast he runs.

　　b.　"What a lovely garden!"

　　　　→ He remarked it was a very lovely garden.

　　c.　"Hello! It's a lovely day today, isn't it?"

　　　　→ He greeted me and said it was a lovely day.

　　d.　"Oh dear! I've got a run in my stockings."

　　　　→ She sighed and said that she had got a run in her stockings.

# 3　時制の一致について

## 3.1　主節と従属節の時制の一致

　時制の一致の基本は，間接話法の伝達動詞が過去形の場合，被伝達部の動詞は現在形→過去形，現在完了形→過去完了形，過去形→過去完了形に変化させます．法助動詞も過去形になります．

　(10)　a.　"What time *is* it?" he asked.

　　b.　He asked what time it *was*.

(11) a. She said to me, "I*'ve* lost my keys."

　　 b. She told me that she *had lost* her keys.

(12) a. She said, "I *saw* Penny at the theatre a couple of days ago."

　　 b. She said she *had seen* Penny at the theatre a couple of days before.

(13) a. I think he *will* be here sooner.

　　 b. I thought he *would* be there sooner.

(14) a. I said to him, "I *shall* be twenty next year."

　　 b. I told him that I *should* be twenty next year.

## 3.2　時制の一致の例外

　時制の一致の原則には，さまざまな例外があります．(15) の例を見てくださ
い．(15a) は，話を伝えた時点 (said＝過去) と事件の起きた時点 (had taken)
とのズレが明らかな例，(15b) は事件の起きた時点と話を伝えた時点がいずれ
も過去で客観的な過去の事実として伝えている例です．(15c) は話を伝えられた
時点が過去であり，話の内容が今でも事実であることを伝えるために現在形を
使っている例，(15d) はこれから行う行動が未来形で表現されて発話時でもま
だ未来の予定であることを示す例です．また，従属節の確定未来の表現が，主節
の時制に合わせて時制の一致を起こす (15e) のような場合や，Columbus が過
去に考えた信念のため過去形 was になる (15f) のような場合もあります．

(15) a. The police **said** that an accident *had taken* place at one of its nu-
clear power stations and admitted that there had been casualties.

　　 b. The police **said** a bomb *went* off between 8:14 and 8:56 just as
millions of Tokyo commuters were returning to their offices after
a three-day holiday weekend.

　　 c. The report **said** that video display terminal work *is* harmful to
pregnant women.

　　 d. U.S. Park Police **said** that an accident reconstruction team *will* be sent out to the site to gather more details on the crash.

e.　I **didn't** realize the match *started* tomorrow.

f.　Columbus **believed** that the earth *was* round.

## 3.3　現在完了形と時制の一致

原則的に，主節の主動詞が現在完了形であれば，被伝達部で時制の一致は起こりません．(16) の被伝達部の時制は直接話法の場合のそれと同じです．しかし，文脈によっては，(17) のように時制の一致が起こります．「…するとよく言っていたが (今も…するつもりかはわからない)」というニュアンスがでます．

(16) a.　I **have** often **said** that I *can't* live without female friends.

b.　I **have** often **said** that I *won't* leave here as long as I live.

c.　People **have** often **said** that politics *has been* the religion of the 20th century.

d.　You **have** often **said** that you yourself *fell* in love with Aunt Caroline.

(17)　Trump **has** often **said** that he *would* make it easier for American corporations like Apple and Google to more easily repatriate earnings.　　　　　[will が has said にあわせて would]

## 3.4　仮定法過去と時制の一致

(18) は仮定法構文で，現在のことを述べていますが，仮定法過去の were, was の時制に合わせて wanted ((18a))，could ((18b))，was ((18c)) が過去形になっていると考えられる例です．

(18) a.　If I **were/was** rich, I would buy you anything you *wanted*.

b.　If I **were** rich, I would try to feed and clothe as many poor people as I *could*.

c.　If I **were** rich, I would tell them exactly what I *was* thinking and not hold back.

# ◉練習問題◉

## 1　以下の日本語を英語に訳しなさい.

1.1　東京スカイツリーはどう行けばいいですか，とよく聞かれる.

1.2　私はタクシーの運転手に道が違うよと言った.

1.3　彼はお父さんが昔は警察官だったと言っていた.

1.4　A:「君は何にする」

　　　B:「ぼくはピザ」

　　　C:「私はコーヒーとサンドウィッチ」

　　　D:「私は水だけで結構」

1.5　A:「奈良公園にはなぜ鹿が多いのですか」

　　　B:「さあ，私にはよく分かりません.」

## 2　以下の英語を日本語に訳しなさい.

2.1　Mr. Yoshida said sadly, "I lost the three-month commuter pass I had just bought."

2.2　When I was buying a ticket from a vending machine, the machine didn't work and I hit it. A station employee came to me and said, "Stop it, will you?"

2.3　According to the traffic report, the outer-loop of Osaka is jammed up.

---

2.4　A: "Why are you late?"

B: "My train broke down at Kyoto Station and didn't move for thirty minutes."

---

2.5　A: "Why are 'torii' painted red?"

B: "Well, I'm not sure, but it may have some religious significance."

---

2.6　I had the flu and went to the doctor. The doctor said I had to get at least eight hours of sleep if I wanted to get well soon.

---

2.7　When I took the exam, I was told that I could use an ordinary pencil, but not a mechanical pencil.

---

2.8　When my children were in elementary school, I took my family on a trip around Canada. Now they scarcely remember visiting there when I tell them the names of those places.

---

# 第6章 準動詞

(『現代高等英文法』pp. 193 〜 225 に該当)

## 1 準動詞の種類

準動詞 (verbal) とは，動詞であると同時に別の働きをかねる非定形 (non-finite) の総称で，(1) にあるように動名詞 (gerund, ING(G))，不定詞 (infinitive)，現在分詞 (present participle, ING(P))，過去分詞 (past participle, PP) があります．

(1) a. *Swimming* is a great sport.　　　　　　　　　　[動名詞]

b. *To meet* him is *to love* him.　　　　　　　　　[不定詞]

c. Two men were *running* alongside a riverbank in the middle of the day.　　　　　　　　　　　　　　　　　[現在分詞]

d. Four languages are officially *recognized* in Switzerland. [過去分詞]

## 2 動名詞

動名詞とは，動詞と名詞の働きをかねる非定形で，動詞の原形に綴り上の変化を加えて ing を付加したものです．動詞のように目的語をとり，副詞に修飾されます．また，意味上の主語をとることもあります．動名詞は，主語，(他動詞・前置詞・一部の形容詞の) 目的語，be 動詞の補語，名詞の同格語の働きをします．否定形は，動名詞の前に not を置きます．

## 2.1 動名詞の用法

### 2.1.1 主語

(2a) は，seeing が主語になっている例です．主語に to 不定詞がくると堅苦しくなり，現代英語では To see is to believe. の形を使うのはまれです．(2b) の動名詞 closing は主語であり，目的語をとっています．(2c) の It は仮主語で，動名詞が真主語です．その動名詞 meeting は you を目的語にとっています．

(2) a. *Seeing* is *believing*.

b. *Closing* the factory means putting people out of work.

c. It's nice *meeting* you.

d. His not *agreeing* to accept the proposals outlined by the committee is baffling.

動名詞の意味上の主語は，(2a, b) のように特定の人の行為でない場合は不要であり，(2c) では話し手が主語なので明示する必要はありません．動名詞の意味上の主語は名詞・代名詞の目的格か所有格で明示されます．例えば (2d) は，代名詞の所有格 his が agreeing の意味上の主語になっています．

(3) の例を見てください．意味上の主語が目的格 (me, Sarah) の場合，第 V 文型になります．my, Sarah's の場合は，my sitting, Sarah's laughing が名詞句になり第 III 文型になります．(4) のように，動名詞が文の主語になると，動名詞の意味上の主語は所有格で表します．(5) のように there 構文の動詞が動名詞化された場合は，there がもとの位置に残ります．

(3) a. Do you mind *me* / *my sitting* here?

b. I'm fed up with *Sarah* / *Sarah's laughing* at my accent.

(4) a. Does *my smoking* annoy you?

b. *Jack's going* to sleep during the wedding was rather embarrassing.

(5) *There* not *being* an index / *There being* no index to that book is a disadvantage.

## ＜もっと詳しく＞　☞『現代高等英文法』p. 196
「to 不定詞との違い」

### 2.1.2　他動詞の目的語

　他動詞は，名詞句，to 不定詞，ING(G)，that 節，wh 節などを目的語にとり，これらの目的語を総称して動詞の補部（complement）と言います．動詞によって取りうる補部が異なり，特に，ING(G) をとるもの，to 不定詞をとるもの，それらの両方をとるものの区別は簡単ではありません．ただし，The sea came rushing in. の rushing は「動詞＋〜ing」ですが，came は自動詞で，rushing は現在分詞 ING(P) と解釈されることから，come は動名詞をとる動詞のリストには含んでいません．また，stop は ING(G) しかとらず，to 不定詞は行動の目的を表す副詞用法である点に注意が必要です．

ING(G) を目的語にとる動詞の一覧：admit, appreciate, avoid, contemplate, delay, deny, dislike, dispute, doubt, dread, enjoy, escape, excuse, favor, finish, finish off, give up, can't help, imagine, include, involve, justify, keep, mean, mention, mind, miss, practice, prevent, propose, quit, recall, recollect, report, resist, risk, stop, suffer, suggest, understand など

上であげる動詞がとる ING(G) は，現実に行われていることや現実に起こることが予測されることを言います．avoid は習慣になっている行為をしないようにする意味であり，stop, give up, finish off などの「停止」に関する意味の動詞は，現実に起こっていること，または，現実に起こると予測されることを停止するのであり，これから起こることを予測するのではありません．

　(6) のように，want, deserve, need の目的語になった ING(G) は，受動の意味になることがあります．

(6) a.　My house *wants repairing*.

b.　Several other points *deserve mentioning*.

c.　My hair *needs cutting*.

### 2.1.3　形容詞の目的語

(7) と (8) の例を見てください．(7) のように，worth は形容詞ですが目的語
をとります．この場合，動名詞の意味上の主語が名詞や代名詞で表されることが
あります．(8) の例では，動名詞が目的格の主語をとっています．

(7)　When you've finished the book, you can tell me if it's *worth* **reading**.

(8) a.　We either have to meet face to face or this deal is just not going to happen and it's not *worth* us **talking** anymore.

　　 b.　If this war is *worth* Americans **fighting** and dying for, …

### 2.1.4　前置詞の目的語

(9) では，前置詞の後には ING (G) が来ています．(10) の前置詞句は，After I had / I finished my homework, … / before you come in / As soon as we arrived at the airport という節と同じ意味で，分詞構文に似た働きをしています．

(9) a.　Thank you for *inviting* me to the party.

　　 b.　I am afraid of *making* mistakes and get very nervous when I speak English.

　　 c.　I have recently begun to doubt whether my own faculties are in danger of *losing* their balance.

(10) a.　After *finishing* my homework, I started reading the novel.

　　 b.　Clean your shoes before *coming* in.

　　 c.　On (《文語》Upon) *arriving* at the airport, we found the passengers had already started boarding.

### 2.1.5　be 動詞の補語

補語をとる自動詞の中で ING (G) を補語にとるものは，be 動詞だけです．補
語に ING (G) をとる場合，主語の名詞の性質が大きく影響します．例えば，
(11), (12) の主語 hobby, pastime, sport は補語には必ず ING (G) が来ます．こ
の is は言い換えの "be" で，主語と補語を入れ替えても意味的には変わりませ

ん．一方，(13) の job は「(職業としての) 仕事，専心すべきこと」の意味では
ING (G) を補語にとりますが，「任務，役割」の意味の job が主語になると to
不定詞をとります．

(11) a.　My hobby is *climbing* mountains.

　　 b.　Her favorite pastime is *singing* karaoke.

(12) a.　My favorite sport is *swimming*.

　　 b.　*Swimming* is my favorite sport.

(13) a.　Your job is *being* a professor and researcher.

　　 b.　The first job is *to decide* who to invite.

　　 c.　The job of the jury is *to assess* the credibility of the witness.


## 2.1.6　名詞の同格

名詞が表す意味内容を説明する際にも動名詞が使われます．(14) の例をあげ
ておきます．

(14) a.　He spent much of his time in later years at his hobby, *growing*
　　　　 plants and flowers.

　　 b.　I remember her happiness *being* around the family and how proud
　　　　 she was of her boys.


## 2.2　完了形の動名詞と動名詞の表す「時」

基本的に，ING (G) は主動詞の「時」と同じです．ING (G) で表される時が主
節の動詞より前のことであることを明示するために，完了形の ING (G) (having
＋PP) を使うことがあります．文脈や状況で，ING (G) の部分が主動詞より前
のできごとであることが自明な場合は，(16) のように完了形の ING (G) は不要
です．

(15) a.　I still feel tired in spite of *having slept* eight hours.

　　 b.　He absolutely denies *having seen* anything, heard anything.

    c.  John is the only one of the students in the class that never admits *having made* a mistake when it is pointed out to him.

    d.  I don't remember *having seen* anyone but him in all the years of my memory.

(16) a.  In spite of *sleeping* longer than usual, she felt tired and a little queasy.

    b.  At first, he denied *seeing* Jennifer.

    c.  Rose admitted *making* illegal bets on football.

    d.  Don't remember *seeing* you before.　　　　　　　　［主語 I の省略］

## 2.3　受動態の動名詞

受動態の ING（G）は，being＋PP の形になります．動名詞の受動態は，(17a, b) のように前置詞の目的語になる場合と，(17c) のように動詞の目的語になる場合があります．

(17) a.  I was honored by *being asked* to give the commencement address on April 18, 2020.

    b.  The safe showed no signs of *having been touched*.

    c.  I remember *being horrified* to see our church completely destroyed by fire.

# 3　不定詞

不定詞（infinitive）は，「主語や時制に対応して形が決まらない場合の動詞の形」の意味で，特に文中で使われる動詞の原形を指して「不定詞」と呼ばれます．

不定詞には，動詞の原形だけからなる原形不定詞（root infinitive／bare infinitive，"do" と表示）と to＋動詞の原形からなる to 不定詞（to-infinitive，"to do" と表示）があります．

「原形」と「原形不定詞」は，前者が動詞の変化の体系（例えば work—works—worked—working）の中の第1番目の変化形（work）のことを指し，後者が文中で使われた動詞の形を指すという点で名称の区別があります．

## 3.1　原形不定詞の用法

　原形不定詞は，動詞や助動詞の後に来ます．(18) の例を見てください．(18a) は，助動詞の後で原形不定詞が使われた例です．(18b) のように，特に話し言葉やくだけた文体では help のような特殊な動詞の後ろにも原形不定詞が来ます．(18c) のような be 動詞の補語の位置では to がよく省かれ，くだけた文体で観察されます．(18d) で使用されている come and＋原形不定詞も口語表現ですが，過去形（came and＋原形不定詞）で使われることはまれです．(18e, f) のように，使役動詞や知覚動詞も補語に原形不定詞をとることがあります．

(18) a. Could you *tell* me where I am?　　　　　[助動詞の後]

　　 b. He helped me (to) *carry* the baggage.　　[help＋目的語の後]

　　 c. My biggest hope now is (to) *go* and see my old friends.

　　　　　　　　　　　　　　　　　　　　　　[be 動詞の補語]

　　 d. Please come and *see* me at six tomorrow evening,

　　　　　　　　　　　　　　　　　　[go and／come and の後]

　　 e. Your smile makes me *feel* happy.　　　[使役動詞の目的格補語]

　　 f. I saw a helicopter *fly* over the mountains.　[知覚動詞の目的格補語]

## ＜もっと詳しく＞　☞『現代高等英文法』p. 204

「know の特殊性」

## 3.2　to 不定詞の用法

　to 不定詞には，名詞，副詞，形容詞の用法があります．名詞用法には，主語，補語，目的語の場合があります．それぞれの例を (19) に示します．(19d) は副

詞用法の例で，文全体を修飾しています．副詞用法の to 不定詞は文のほかにも，
節全体，形容詞，動詞，副詞を修飾する場合があります．(19e) は形容詞用法の
例で，名詞を修飾していますが，後でみるように，名詞と to 不定詞の関係は多
様です．

(19) a. *To know* is one thing; *to do* is another. 　　　　　　[名詞用法，主語]

　　 b. My plan is *to hire* a car when I arrive in America and travel
　　　　 about. 　　　　　　　　　　　　　　　　　　　　[名詞用法，補語]

　　 c. We were hoping *to see* you today. 《丁寧》 　　　　[名詞用法，目的語]

　　 d. *To tell* the truth, sometimes your ideas are better than my original
　　　　 ones. 　　　　　　　　　　　　　　　　　　　　　　[副詞用法]

　　 e. Maine is a great state and a very nice place *to live*. 　[形容詞用法]

　to 不定詞の意味上の主語は，(20) のように一般的に for … で表し，それがな
いときは，文の主語あるいは不特定の人が不定詞の主語です．目的語＋to do を
とる動詞の場合，不定詞の意味上の主語はその目的語です．(21b) は「人に…し
てもらいたい」という話し手の意思を表す意思動詞で，意味上の主語は動詞 like
の目的語の you です．

(20) a. It is difficult **for me** *to memorize* all the words in a day.

　　 b. It is impossible (**for anyone**) *to live* alone on the Antarctic.

　　 c. I love *to swim* in the ocean in summer.

(21) a. I'd like *to visit* your country some time.

　　 b. I'd like **you** *to come* and visit us some time.

### 3.2.1　名詞用法

**3.2.1.1**　主語

　(22) のように一般的に to 不定詞を主語にすると堅苦しい表現になるため，そ
れを避けて通常，仮主語を使って (23) のようにします．(23a) のように to 不
定詞の意味上の主語が明示されていない場合，一般の人が主語になります．
(23b) では不定詞の意味上の主語は of him で，形容詞が人の評価を言う場合に

は of が選ばれます．(23c) では完了不定詞が未実現の過去の出来事を仮定する
仮定法の条件節，主節が仮定法の帰結節の形になっており，(23d) と同じ意味
になります．to 不定詞の名詞用法と言われる用法は，本来的な名詞の性質とは
かなり違った特徴をもっています．

(22) a. *To wait* for people who were late made him angry.　《文語》

　　 b. *To understand* the situation completely requires more thought than
　　　　he has given so far.　《文語》

(23) a. *It is* interesting *to know* how English has come to be used all over
　　　　the world.

　　 b. *It was* inconsiderate of him not *to tell* us of his decision to call
　　　　off the party.

　　 c. *It would have been* a lot of fun *to have gone* to Africa with him.

　　 d. If you had gone to Africa with him, it would have been a lot of
　　　　fun.

## ＜もっと詳しく＞　☞『**現代高等英文法**』p. 207
「to 不定詞の名詞用法の「名詞の度合い」」

　to 不定詞の否定は，not to ～ のように to の前に not が来るのが原則ですが，
(24) のように to not ～ になる場合もあります．

(24) a. I try *to not get* annoyed.

　　 b. The point is *to not let* others control you.

　　 c. He chose *to not make* a fuss and just let JFK go on to be president.

### 3.2.1.2　be 動詞の補部
　主語の名詞によって，補語に来るものが決定されることがあります．例えば
(25), (26) のように，mistake, dream は，補語に to 不定詞を取ります．この種
の名詞のリストは，PART III 第 1 章にあげています．mistake の補部に来る to
不定詞は過去の行為を表しており，dream の補語に来る to 不定詞は未来の行為

を表しています．(25a), (26a) とも be 動詞が言い換えの be であるため, (25b),
(26b) のように主語と補部を入れ替えても，意味に大きな違いはありません．ま
た，仮主語の it を使って (25c), (26c) のようにすることもできます．

(25) a. **Your mistake** was *to write* him that letter.

   b. *To write* him that letter was **your mistake**.

   c. It was **your mistake** *to write* him that letter.

(26) a. **My dream** is *to find* a cure for cancer.

   b. *To find* a cure for cancer is **my dream**.

   c. It is **my dream** *to find* a cure for cancer.

the only thing she does, the important thing we do, the last thing he did, the
best thing they did のような表現は，補語に to 不定詞を従えます．そのほかに
what（擬似分裂文）(PART II 第 1 章) と all が同じ用法を持っています．

(27) a. The only thing I could do was simply *to escape*.

   b. All I wanted to do was *to get* to know what it was like to be a
normal girl.

   c. What they were trying to do was *to get* him to make an error.

(28) は He is a person for us to blame. から a person for us が省略されたも
のです．(29) も同様に This letter is a letter to tell … から a letter が省略され
たものです．(28), (29) の to 不定詞は省略された名詞句を修飾する形容詞的修
飾語です．また to 不定詞は，実現されなかったことを表現する (30) の完了不
定詞（perfect infinitive）でも使われます．

(28) He is *to blame*.

(29) This letter is *to tell* you that you've done a good job.

(30) My original plan was *to have* roasted turkey but I changed my mind
at the last minute.

### 3.2.1.3　動詞の目的語

動詞の補部の種類には，(31) のように目的語の位置に to 不定詞を直接取る場

合，「目的語＋to 不定詞」をとる場合，「疑問詞＋to 不定詞」をとる場合があります．

(31) a. Couldn't you have managed *to say* something nice about the meal?
b. I'd hate *you to think* I didn't appreciate what you'd done.
c. I'm just wondering *what to say* to you.

補部の種類に分けて動詞をリストすると以下のようになります．

to 不定詞を目的語にとる動詞：can't afford, agree, aim, arrange, begin, bother, would you care, claim, decide, demand, determine, expect, fail, would hate / hate, hope, intend, learn, would like / like, long, love, manage, mean, offer, prepare, pretend, proceed, swear, trouble, volunteer, want, wish など

＼！注意！￣￣￣￣￣￣￣￣￣￣￣￣￣￣￣￣￣￣￣￣

　to 不定詞はこれから行う予定の行動の意味になっていることが多く，意志・願望を表す expect, hope, intend, mean, think, want は，完了形の不定詞を従えて実現されなかったことを表します．

目的語＋to 不定詞をとる動詞：advise, allow, appoint, ask, assist, cause, challenge, charge, command, direct, drive, enable, encourage, expect, force, get, would hate, help, influence, instruct, intend, invite, lead, leave, would like / like, love, mean, need, order, permit, persuade, prefer, pressure, promise, prompt, recommend, remind, request, require, *show, teach, *tell, trouble, want, warn, wish (* を付けた動詞は通例「目的語＋how to 不定詞」の形をとる) など

疑問詞＋to 不定詞をとる動詞：arrange, ask, check, choose, consider, decide, discover, discuss, establish, explain, find out, forget, imagine, judge, know, learn, notice, observe, remember, say, see, show, tell など

ING (G) も to 不定詞もとる動詞：begin, continue, forget, hate, intend, would like, would love, prefer, start など

> **！注意！**
>
> これらの動詞が ING(G) をとる場合は一般的なこと，to 不定詞は特定の
> ことを言う場合に好まれます．また，remember, forget, regret, try が to 不
> 定詞をとる場合は未完の行為，ING(G) は過去の行為を言うのに使われま
> す．この場合，ING(G) が having PP になることもあります．(32), (33)
> の例を見て確認してください．

(32) a. I hate *to be* delayed.

  b. I hate *being* delayed.

(33) a. I must remember *to ask* him.

  b. I remember *seeing / having seen* her when she was a student.

### 3.2.2 副詞用法

to 不定詞のなかでも，節（文）または語句（形容詞，動詞，副詞）を修飾する
ものを副詞用法と言います．(34) のようにフレーズや目的を表す用法で使われ
て文全体を修飾するもの，形容詞を修飾してその理由・原因を述べるもの，結果
を表すもの，準法助動詞の働きをする「be + 形容詞 + to」が to 不定詞の副詞用
法です．

(34) a. *To be frank with you*, you are wrong.　　　　　［文副詞のフレーズ］

  b. *To look your best* at all times, keep your clothes neat and your
    person clean.

    ［文副詞，目的の意味（= in order to do, so as to do で目的の意味が強まる）］

  c. I am glad *to see you*.　　　　　　　　　　　　　［語副詞，原因］

  d. His father lived *to be* 94 years old.　　　　　　　［語副詞，結果］

  e. The bridge was too narrow for the truck *to cross*.　［語副詞，結果］

  f. She sounded very eager *to see* you.

    ［準法助動詞として働く be + 形容詞 + to, be の代わりに sound］

### 3.2.3 形容詞用法

形容詞用法とは，名詞の直後に来て，その名詞の意味を限定したり，叙述したり，説明を加えたりする to 不定詞のことを言います．(35) の例を見てください．名詞と直後に来ている to 不定詞の関係はさまざまです．(35a) では，the only person が do it の主語となっています．(35b) では，a large family が support の目的語です．(35c) では，no house が live in の目的語になっています．(35d) では，本来 buy food or water **with** money の関係なので，money to buy food or water **with** となるはずですが，money などの特定の名詞は前置詞を削除して使います．このような前置詞を削除した構文で使われる特定の名詞には，道具・手段の名詞 (device, instrument, job, means, measure, money, power, ticket)，時 (age, date, hour, leave, leisure, moment, time)，場所 (place, position, room (余地), situation, space) などがあります．(35e) は，「have, give などの意味の軽い動詞 + 名詞 + to do」のように使われる軽動詞構文 (light verb construction) です．(35f) は，he is able to speak English を名詞化した形 (his ability to speak English) で，(35f) は he refused to pay ... を名詞化した形 (his refusal to pay ...) です．

(35) a. He is the only person *to do* it.　　　　　　　　　[主語]

　　 b. He has a large family *to support*.　　　　　　　　[目的語]

　　 c. They have no house *to live* in.　　　　　　　　[前置詞の目的語]

　　 d. We have no money *to buy* food or water.　　　　[前置詞削除構文]

　　 e. Give me a chance *to speak*.　　　　　　　　　　[軽動詞構文]

　　 f. Everybody praises his ability *to speak* English.

　　　　　　　　　　　　　　　　　　　　　　[形容詞由来の名詞の補部]

　　 g. His refusal *to pay* the fine got him into even more trouble.

　　　　　　　　　　　　　　　　　　　　　　[動詞由来の名詞の補部]

## 3.3 完了不定詞の用法

完了不定詞 (to have + PP) には，(36) のように名詞用法で実現しなかったこ

とを表現する用法と，(37) のように主節の時より前の出来事を表す副詞用法が
あります．

(36) a. It would have been a lot of fun *to have gone* to Africa with him.

　　　　　　　　　　　　　　　　　　　　　　　　［主語になる，仮定］

　　 b. My original plan was *to have roasted* turkey but I changed my
mind at the last minute.　　　［be 動詞の補語で，実現しなかった過去］

　　 c. I meant *to have given* you a call, but I couldn't find time to do
so.　　　　　　　　　　　　　［動詞の目的語で，実現しなかった過去］

(37) a. I am glad *to have met* you.　　　［原因，主節の時より前に起きたこと］

　　 b. I'm happy *to have found* a recipe that pleases him.

　　　　　　　　　　　　　　　　　　　［原因，主節の時より前に起きたこと］


# 4　分詞

　分詞 (participle) とは，動詞の機能に形容詞的な機能（名詞を修飾する）が加
わったもので，動名詞と同じ形の現在分詞 (present participle, ING(P)) と，過
去分詞 (past participle, PP) があります．


## 4.1　現在分詞

　現在分詞は，be 動詞と共に進行形をつくる (38a)，名詞を修飾する (38b)，
知覚動詞・使役動詞の補語（目的格補語とも言う）で使われる (38c, d)，形容
詞・名詞の後に来て意味を補足する (38e) のように使われます．

(38) a. Time is *running* out!　　　　　　　　　　　　　　　　　［進行形］

　　 b. Marie looked at the *sleeping* baby.　　　　　　　　　　［名詞の修飾］

　　 c. I saw a dog *lying* on the street.　　　　　　　　　［知覚動詞の補語］

　　 d. My clumsy mistake set all the girls *giggling*.　　　　［使役動詞の補語］

　　 e. We are all busy *preparing* for Christmas.　　　　［形容詞の意味の補足］

    f.  I'd love to go *shopping*.　　　　　　　　　　[go -ing の構文]

    g.  *Pointing* at my forehead he asked if I had been fighting. [分詞構文]

　名詞を前位修飾する現在分詞は，(39a) のように名詞の前に来て，ストレスは名詞と現在分詞の両方に置かれます．一方，(39b) の複合名詞の場合は，ストレスは現在分詞に置かれます．修飾する現在分詞が補足要素を伴って長い場合には，(40) のように名詞を後ろから修飾します．

(39)  a.  ˈrunning ˈwater / a ˈsleeping ˈbaby / a ˈdying ˈsoldier

　　　　　　　　　　　　　　　　[前位修飾，単独の名詞を修飾]

    b.  a ˈwalking stick / a ˈboiling point / a ˈswimming race / a ˈsmoking room / fanatically ˈcheering crowds　　　　　　[複合名詞]

(40)  a.  Do you know the boy *running over there*?　　　[後位修飾]

    b.  The number of children *needing help* has increased 30 percent since last year.　　　　　　　　　　　　[後位修飾]

　(41) は知覚動詞の第 V 文型の用法，使役動詞 get, have, keep, leave, set も (42) のような第 V 文型の用法で使われます．

(41)  a.  I found him *dozing* at his desk.

    b.  Rocks were seen *falling* from the cliffs.

(42)  a.  He left me *waiting* outside.

    b.  How can we get things *moving*?

be busy, be careful, have difficulty, not be long, be successful, have a hard time などの後で，意味の補足をする現在分詞の用法があります．(43) を見てみましょう．about, in などの前置詞をとる場合は，動名詞です．

(43)  a.  Be careful *driving* home.

    b.  Some children have great difficulty (in) *learning* how to spell.

    c.  He won't be long time (in) *getting* there.

(44) のように there's NP の後に現在分詞が来て，NP を説明する用法もあり

ます.

(44)　There's a person *waiting* to see you in the drawing room.

(38f) で示した go＋ING (P) のように, ING (P) が動詞句の後に来て意味の補足をする付帯状況の分詞構文の用法もあります. go のほか, come, spend time／money, waste time／money に同様の用法があります.

(45) a.　Jess **came** *flying* around the corner and banged straight into me.
　　　b.　They **spent about £600** just *rebuilding* the front porch.
　　　c.　He **wasted a whole afternoon** *trying* to repair the car.

　分詞によって節と同じ働きをする構文を, 分詞構文 (participial construction) と言います. 主節の主語と分詞の主語が同じ場合は分詞の主語は省きますが, (46) のように主語が異なる場合はそれを残します. (46) は, 主節より前の時を表すために使われた完了形の場合です. 受動形の場合は being になりますが, being はよく省略されて過去分詞による分詞構文になります. 否定の not の位置は分詞の前に置かれます.

(46)　The lights *having* gone out, we couldn't see a thing.
　　　(cf. As the lights had gone out, we couldn't see a thing.)
(47) a.　*Introduced* last year by the Ministry of Health, the ban forbade doctors to perform the operation.　　　［過去分詞による分詞構文］
　　　b.　*Not knowing* what to do, she applied to me for advice.
　　　　　　　　　　　　　　　　　　　　　　　　　［否定の分詞構文］

## ＜もっと詳しく＞　☞『現代高等英文法』p. 220
「being の省略」

## 4.2　分詞構文の意味

　分詞構文は,「時」「理由」「結果」「条件」「付帯状況」の意味で使われます.

以下の (48) を見てみましょう.

(48) a.　Mike hurt his hand *playing* badminton.　　　　　　[時]
　　　　　( = when he was playing badminton)

　　b.　They dumped the waste into the river, *killing* all the fish.　[結果]
　　　　　( = and killed all the fish)

　　c.　We plan to eat outside, weather *permitting*.　　　　[条件]
　　　　　( = if weather permits)

　　d.　She stood still for a few seconds, *looking* around and then down
　　　　at the water. ( = and looked around)　　　　　　[付帯状況]

また，分詞構文と主節の意味関係を明確にするために，(49) のように分詞の
前に接続詞を置く場合があります.

(49) a.　**While** *sleeping*, I fell out of the bed.

　　b.　**After** *finishing* my undergraduate degree at the University of Tex-
　　　　as at San Antonio, I went to the John Marshall Law School in
　　　　Chicago.

2 つの節の主語が違う場合，分詞構文の主語を明示するのが原則ですが，誤解
を生じなければ (50a) のように主語が省略された独立分詞構文 (absolute participial construction) が使われます. 前置詞のように働く following, considering,
regarding や会話でよく使われるフレーズ having said that などは，もとは独立
分詞構文です.

(50) a.　When *adjusting* the machine, the electric supply should be discon-
　　　　nected.

　　b.　*Following* the lecture, we were able to ask questions.

　　c.　He forgets most things, but *having said that*, he always remem-
　　　　bers my birthday.

## 5 過去分詞

過去分詞には，have + PP で完了形を作る (51a)，受動形を作る (51b)，完了または受身の意味になり名詞を前位修飾する (51c)，第 V 文型で生じる使役動詞・知覚動詞の目的格補語で使われる (51d, e)，分詞構文として使われる (51f)といった特徴が見られます.

(51) a. Spring has *come*. [完了形]

　　 b. He was *promoted* to a general manager in 1997. [受動形]

　　 c. There could be a *broken* bone beneath the swelling. [名詞修飾]

　　 d. The neighbors had him *arrested*. [使役動詞 + O + PP]

　　 e. He felt his eyes *dazzled* by a blaze of light. [知覚動詞 + O + PP]

　　 f. *Given* the opportunity, he will make an excellent teacher. [分詞構文]

過去分詞が，形容詞として使われる場合があります. このように形容詞化されたものは，一般的に特殊な意味で使われることから過去分詞と区別できることが多くあります. 形容詞化した considered が，限定用法と叙述用法で使われた例 (52) を見てみましょう.

(52) a. He hadn't had time to form a *considered* opinion.

　　 b. I think Australia is acting in our national interest, we are very careful and very *considered* in that approach.

過去分詞は，名詞を前位修飾します. 受動の意味の場合と完了の意味の場合があります. 前位修飾では (54) のように，「-ly 副詞 + PP + 名詞」になります.

(53) He is a *retired* teacher. [完了の意味]

(54) a. She showed me a beautifully *painted* picture. [受動の意味]

　　 b. freshly *baked* bread / federally *owned* land / a densely *populated* area / visually *handicapped* children / genetically *modified* organisms / a finely *chopped* onion.

(55) は過去分詞が補部を伴っていることから, 名詞を後位修飾します. また, 分詞の補部が明らかな場合, (56) のように省略されることがあります.

(55) a.   The generation *born* forty years ago is taking the rein.

   b.   Those are the sleds *used* by Innuits.

(56)   Unfortunately, we cannot answer all questions *submitted*.

[by the audience などの省略]

過去分詞の分詞構文では, φ の部分に being が省略されていると考えられます.

(57) a.   Once  φ  *opened*, the contents should be consumed within three days.                                            [独立分詞構文]

   (cf. Once the bag is *opened*, … → Once the bag *being opened*, … → Once *opened*, …)

   b.   She dashed into the rain, her head  φ  *protected* only by a thin scarf.                                         [独立分詞構文]

   c.   His face  φ  *unshaven*, his coat  φ  torn, and with no shoes on, he presented a very unkempt appearance.          [独立分詞構文]

# ⦿練習問題⦿

## 1 次の英文を日本語訳しなさい.

1.1 My son has been studying since this morning though it is a holiday today. I wish he would play tennis or something.

---

1.2 I went to an alumni meeting of my high school last Sunday. It really was worth going to. We had lively talks after not seeing each other for three years.

---

1.3 Many companies adopt the so-called lifetime-employment system, so that new employees usually expect to keep working for the same company till their retirement.

---

1.4 Because of the recent depression in the American car industry, many workers were laid off.

1.5 The survey conducted by the teachers shows that eighty percent of the students want to go to college.

---

1.6 Opposition parties are virtually powerless and the Liberal-Democratic Party has been in power for a long time.

---

1.7　"What is the voting age in Japan?"

"It is eighteen."

"It's the same in America.  It's legal to drive after sixteen and drink and smoke after twenty-one in most states."

_____

_____

_____

## 2　次の日本語を，（　　）の語句を使用して英語に訳しなさい.

2.1　明日の授業の準備ができた. (finish)

_____

2.2　わからない単語が出てきたら辞書を見るよりしかたない. (all you can do is … / look it up)

_____

2.3　あそこでうたた寝している老人を知っていますか. (doze)

_____

2.4　窓を開けていただけますか. (mind)

_____

2.5　彼は事故で脚を折った. (get)

_____

2.6　映画を見に行くのが趣味だ. (enjoy going)

_____

2.7　魚が焦げてるにおいがする. (smell)

_____

2.8　英字新聞をとりたいのですが. (subscribe)

_____

PART
III

品詞を中心として

# 第1章　名詞と冠詞

（『現代高等英文法』pp. 228 ～ 261, pp. 280 ～ 290 に該当）

## 1　名詞

　名詞（noun）とは，世界に存在する，または想像上の事物・概念・状態などに与えられた名前です．次々に発明される新しい物や新発見にも名前が与えられますので，名詞は増えていきます．

　名詞の多くは単数形・複数形をもち，修飾語を伴って文の主語や補語，目的語となります．book はそのままで使われることは少なく，a book / the book / two books / those interesting books / the book that she wrote のように，冠詞，数詞，指示代名詞，形容詞，後置修飾語などを伴って使われます．このような名詞を中心としたまとまりを名詞句（noun phrase, 略称 NP）と呼びます．Tom のような単独で使われる固有名詞も名詞句になります．

## 2　名詞の複数形

　名詞の複数形には，-s / -es をつけて規則変化するもの，不規則変化するもの，外来語に由来する複数形を作るものの3種類があります．

Table 3.1.1　名詞の複数形

| 規則変化<br>(-s / es) | book－books / ship－ships / desk－desks など<br>dish－dishes / glass－glasses / watch－watches など |
|---|---|
| 不規則変化 | 音とつづりが変わるもの：foot－feet / louse－lice / mouse－mice / man－men など<br>-en がつくもの：child－children / ox－oxen など<br>変化しないもの：sheep－sheep / deer－deer など |
| 外来語複数 | datum－data / thesis－theses / criterion－criteria / tempo－tempi など |

**！注意！**

(1) o で終わる単語は -s をつけるものと -es をつけるもの，両方あるものがあります：photo－photos / tomato－tomatoes；volcano－volcanos－volcanoes など.

(2) -s / -es が付くと語末の無声子音が有声化するものがあります：house－houses / leaf－leaves など.

# 3　名詞の種類と振る舞い

　伝統的に，普通名詞（common noun，例：book, dog, desk），集合名詞（mass noun，例：family, nation, elite），抽象名詞（abstract noun，例：beauty, courage, democracy），固有名詞（proper noun，例：Japan, Mary, Europe），物質名詞（material noun，例：oil, iron, water）に分類されます.

## 3.1　普通名詞・物質名詞・抽象名詞の可算・不可算

(1) a.　There's *a fish* swimming in the river.

　　b.　I don't like *fish* nor pork.

(2) a.  Do you like *coffee*?

  b.  A wide range of *coffees* are now available.

(3)   He showed great *courage* and *determination*.

(4) a.  It was *a kindness* you've shown me, letting me meet them.

  b.  He did me *many kindnesses* while I was in London.

(5) a.  She looked up in *surprise*.

  b.  In *a surprise*, coach Tommy Tuberville announced that Chris Peery will be rejoining the squad.

  c.  I have so *many surprises* waiting for you.

　可算か不可算かというのは，名詞の重要な機能的特徴です．可算名詞（countable noun）は a/an という不定冠詞がつくといった特徴があります．また，one, two, three … と数えられます．不可算名詞（uncountable noun）は a/an はつきませんし，one, two, three … と数えられません．名詞の中には (1), (2) のように可算名詞，不可算名詞の両方で使われるものが多くあります．fish は可算名詞が基本ですが，魚肉という物質名詞になると不可算名詞になります．coffee は飲み物としては物質名詞で数えられませんが，コーヒーの種類をいうときは可算名詞になります．喫茶店で Two *coffees*, please. のようにも使われます．(3) は不可算名詞としてだけ使われるものです．不可算名詞の中には (4) のように two, three … と数えられないのに a や many などとは共起する名詞があります．

　(5a) の名詞 surprise は，不可算名詞として「驚き」という意味を表す抽象名詞です．(5b) の In a surprise は「突然」の意味です．この意味の surprise は a が付きますが，×in surprises のように複数名詞にはなりません．「驚かせるために計画したサプライズ」の意味では a surprise, two surprises と数えられますので，可算名詞です．抽象名詞には，① a もとらず複数形にもならない courage のようなもの，② a もとるし複数形にもなるが，数えられない kindness のようなもの，③「サプライズ」のように a もとるし複数形にもなるし数えられるもの，があります．このような可算，不可算の概念は，英語母語話者の具象と抽象の感覚が反映したものです．

## 3.2　可算・不可算と具象・抽象

同じ名詞でも，a がつくかつかないかで別の意味を表すことがあります．
glass（ガラス）—a glass（グラス）/ ice（氷）—an ice（アイスクリーム）/ iron（鉄）
—an iron（アイロン）/ paper（紙）—a paper（論文）など

## ＜もっと詳しく＞　☞『現代高等英文法』p. 233
「なぜ mashed potatoes か」

## 3.3　同義の別単語で可算・不可算の区別

　同じ「旅行」の意味でも，travel は抽象名詞です．trip, journey, excursion は
具体的な1回の「旅行」を言うので，可算名詞です．

(6)　We share a love of literature, food and *travel*.
(7)　We went on *a trip* to the mountain.
(8)　We had *a long journey* ahead of us.
(9)　They've gone on *an excursion* to York.

このような同義の単語の可算・不可算の区別は次のようなペアに見られます．
bread—a loaf / clothing—a garment / laughter—a laugh / luggage—a bag /
poetry—a poem / work—a job

## 3.4　集合名詞

(10)　My *family* are very healthy and sport-oriented.
(11)　My *family* is from Tripoli.

　集合名詞は，捉え方によって単数として扱うか，複数として扱うかが決まりま
す．家の一人ひとりを意識すると複数扱いですが，家族をひとまとまりとして扱
うと単数扱いとなります．このような集合名詞には以下のようなものがあります．

audience, class, club, committee, company, crew, crowd, elite, family, government, group, union など

The BBC のような会社名や団体名も単数扱いする場合と複数扱いする場合があります．

# 4　不可算名詞の数え方

不可算名詞自体は数えられませんが，容器や重量，長さなどの単位で数えることができます．基本的に「a A of 不可算名詞」という形になります．この A のところに生じる，不可算名詞を数える手段となるものを部分詞（partitive）ということがあります．a bar of chocolate / two bars of chocolate では bar が部分詞です．

(12)　She bought **two bars** of *chocolate* at the supermarket.
(13)　Father often says that nothing can beat **a mug** of *beer* after playing tennis.
(14)　There aren't **many pieces** of *furniture* in his room.
(15)　I need **two sheets** of *white paper*.

部分詞を使った言い方の中には a bar of chocolate → a chocolate bar / a lump of sugar → a sugar lump のように意味的に対応する表現を持つものもあります．a mug of beer「ビール一杯」/ a beer mug「ひとつのビールジョッキ」ではこのような対応関係がありません．

　日本語では数えられそうなものでも英語では不可算名詞なので，a piece of ... で数えるものがあります．a piece of furniture / a piece of work / a piece of research / a piece of nonsense / a piece of music / a piece of information / a piece of advice / a piece of news などがそうです．

Table 3.1.2　部分詞の一覧

| 抽象名詞 | *a bit of* advice／*a bit of* knowledge／*a bit of* fun／*a stroke of* luck／*a spell of* bad weather／*a spell of* work／*a period of* calm |
|---|---|
| 物質名詞 | *a ball of* wool／*a chunk of* change《俗語》大金／*a pile of* laundry／*a piece of* iron |
| 食品 | *a piece of* cheese／*a piece of* bread／*a piece of* cake／*a loaf of* bread／a *dash of* salt／*a drop of* water／*a lump of* sugar／*a ton of* wheat／*a cup of* wheat／*a barrel of* flour／*a spoonful of* flour／*a pack of* flour／*a teaspoon of* sugar／*a pinch of* sugar／*a cup of* sauce／*a bowl of* sauce／*a jar of* sauce／*a can of* pepper／*a grinding of* pepper／*a dash of* pepper |
| 集団・群れ | *a pack of* wolves／*a pack of* dogs／*a herd of* sheep／*a herd of* elephants／*a bunch of* people／*a majority of* people／*a flock of* birds／*a swarm of* bees／*a school of* fish／*an army of* frogs |

## ＜もっと詳しく＞　☞『現代高等英文法』p. 236

「a good cup of coffee などの表現」

# 5　固有名詞

　固有名詞はその名前で呼ばれる人や物を指します．複数形になる場合や a を伴って普通名詞になる場合があります．

(16)　I know *several Mr Wilsons*.

(17)　He was a close friend of *the Kennedys*.

(18)　A man called Wilson murdered *a Mrs Henrichson* because she refused to rent him a room.

# 6　名詞型

　動詞型と同じように，名詞も意味に応じて名詞型（noun pattern）をとるものがあります．名詞型では，どのような主語をとるのか，どのような動詞と結合するのかといった観点も重要です．名詞型を考えていく際には，その名詞が名詞型とは関係のない内容名詞なのか，名詞型の形に関係するトピック名詞，叙述名詞なのかということに留意する必要があります．I asked God to give me a happy *dream.* では dream は名詞型とは関係のない内容名詞です．一方，下の（20）でみるように，My *dream* is to do. / It is my *dream* to do. のような名詞型を指定する dream はトピック名詞です．以下ではトピック名詞を NP (topic)，叙述名詞を NP (pred.) と表記しています．

(19) a. *My understanding* was **that we were to meet here**.

[NP (topic) is that … ]

　　 b. **It was** *my understanding* **that we were to meet here**.

[it is NP (topic) that … ]

(20) a. *My dream* is **to sing like her**.　　　　[NP (topic) is to do]

　　 b. **It is** *my dream* **to sing like her**.　　　[it is NP (topic) to do]

(21) **It's** *a pity* **that you can't stay longer**.　　[it is NP (pred.) that … ]

(22) **It's** *a shame* **to be so wasteful**.　　　[it is NP (pred.) to do]

　トピック名詞と叙述名詞の違いは，主語と補語を入れ替えられるかということにあります．トピック名詞である understanding は，My understanding was that … → That … was my understanding → It was my understanding that … という変形が可能ですが，叙述名詞では，×A pity is that … / ×A shame is to do のような形を使うことはできません．叙述名詞は that 節や to 不定詞の内容が話し手にとって何であるかを述べる形容詞的性質を持っているためです．

　同じ名詞でもトピック名詞になったり，叙述名詞になったりするものもあります．例えば The fact is that … では fact はトピック名詞ですが，It is a fact that … の fact は叙述名詞です．

hobby や book, desk, coffee などは内容名詞なので補語に that 節や to 不定詞などの名詞型を指定する働きは持っていません．したがって My hobby is photograph / collecting stamps. のように名詞や動名詞を取るのが英語らしい表現で，My hobby is to collect stamps. とは言いません．

## 6.1 It is NP (topic) that … / NP (topic) is that … の名詞型

(23) *The fact* is **that** science is never based on certainty because it is inductive.

(24) *The reason* these cars are so expensive is **that** they are largely built by hand.

(25) *My view* is **that** we don't know what's causing climate change on this planet.

(26) *My mother's hope* is **that** I will marry Jones.

これらの文はいずれも It is the fact / the reason / my view / my mother's hope that … の名詞型にすることができます．

トピック名詞には以下のようなものがあります．

advantage, answer, assumption, belief, consensus, concern, conclusion, consideration, criticism, difference, difficulty, evidence, expectation, fact, finding, hint, hope, idea, impression, message, news, problem, proposal, reason, result, rumor, theory, trouble, wish など

一部のトピック名詞は，that 節の中に仮定法現在を取ります．このようなトピック名詞には，claim, decision, idea, insistence, intention, suggestion, wish などがあります．

(27) **It was** *his wish* **that** she have it.

(28) **It was** *his idea* **that** I join the club.

The trouble is that … / The fact is that … などの表現では，the が省略された

り，さらに Trouble/Fact is, ... のように that を省略し，カンマを置くこともあ
ります.

(29)　*Trouble is* nobody is aware of this.

(30)　*Fact is*, they are lovers of classical music.

### ＜もっと詳しく＞　☞『現代高等英文法』p. 244
「The truth is that ... の名詞型と truth の取る同格 that 節」

## 6.2　It is NP (topic) to do / NP (topic) is to do の名詞型

(31)　**It is** *my desire* **to have** a house in the suburbs.

(32)　**It is** *our hope* **to go** to Europe on our honeymoon.

(33)　**It was** *his motion* **to take** a walk.

(34)　*The goal* **is to make** people very comfortable when they enter the
building.

(35)　*The idea* **is to promote** healthy eating.

(36)　*Our job* **is to govern** with a sense of responsibility.

(37)　*Our aim* **is to get** our babies and adults educated.

　この形を取るトピック名詞には，目的や役割などの行動に関わる意味を持ちま
す．このような名詞には以下のようなものがあります．

advice, aim, answer, business, claim, desire, dream, goal, intention, job, mis-
sion, plan, proposal, responsibility, solution など

## 6.3　It is NP (pred.) that ... / It is NP (pred.) to do の名詞型

　It is NP (pred.) that ... の名詞型は，that 節で述べられる命題に対する話し手
の判断を表します．It is NP (pred.) to do の名詞型は to 不定詞で表された行為
に対する話し手の判断を表します．話し手の判断を述べるので，いずれの場合も

It is NP (pred.) の部分は法表現の一種です.

(38) **It is** *a pity* **that** you cannot come with us.

(39) **It is** *a shame* **that** you couldn't complete your assignment for the summer.

(40) **It's** *a mercy* she wasn't seriously hurt.

(41) **It's** *a marvel* **that** he stays right at the precipice.

(42) **It is** *a sin* **to tell** a lie.

(43) **It's** *no inconvenience* **to drive** you to the station.

(44) **It was** *a big mistake* **to leave** my umbrella at home.

(45) **It was** *a good idea* **to plant** those trees.

It is NP(pred.) that ... の名詞型を取る叙述名詞には certainty, coincidence, fact, marvel, mercy, miracle, myth, pity, reality, shame などがあります. 一方, It is NP(pred.) to do の名詞型を取る叙述名詞には, challenge, comfort, crime, fallacy, idea, inconvenience, joy, lie, misnomer, mistake, pleasure, privilege, relief, sin, thrill, tradition などがあります.

## 6.4 have / give / do NP to do / that 節の構文

軽動詞の have / give / do はさまざまな名詞を目的語にとって, 全体でひとつの動詞のような役割をすることがあります. これらの表現のあとに to do / that 節を取ることも多くあります.

(46) have NP to do / give 人 NP to do

a. He *had the kindness to show* us around.

b. This *gave me the opportunity to see* my brother from a different perspective.

have NP to do の to do は文の主語が行う行為を表します. give 人 NP to do の形では to do は目的語の人が行う行為を表します. 本来的に人が持っているものは have の形を取り, 人に与えることができるものは give の形が可能になり

ます.

　この形を取るものには以下のような名詞があります. have と give の両方を取れるものについては * をつけています.

authority*, capacity*, chance*, courage*, disposition, duty*, experience*, freedom*, genius, gift*, grace, kindness, opportunity*, pains, reason*, right* など

(47)　have NP that 節
　　a.　Do you *have any expectation that* the plan will be successful?
　　b.　I *had the impression that* it was all done in a hurry.

　この形では that 節は名詞と同格で名詞の内容を説明します. この形を取るものには以下のようなものがあります.

attitude, belief, confidence, expectation, faith, feeling, idea, impression, knowledge, notion, realization, thought など

(48)　have NP of / for / in doing
　　a.　He *has a preference for watching* TV to reading novels.
　　b.　We *have no hope of finding* him.
　　c.　I *have no interest in going* abroad now.

　この形には have the advantage of, have no clue of, have concern about / over, have every confidence in, have no evidence in, have a feeling of, have a suspicion of, have a sense of などがあります.

(49)　do a / the / one's N
　　a.　I'll *do my best* to be a better person in this new year.
　　b.　He's learned how to *do the dishes*, put on a load of washing and pack his own lunch.

　この形には, do one's best, do the cleaning, do the dishes, do one's duty, do an exercise, do a favor, do the washing, do one's work などがあります.

(50)　give / make / take / have a N

    a.　She *gave a sigh* of relief.

    b.　Excuse me, I have to *make a phone call.*

    c.　Let's *take a ten-minute break.*

    d.　She *had a hot drink* and went to bed.

　動作などを表す名詞が軽動詞と結合してひとつの動詞のような意味を表すことがあります．その場合，動詞よりも意味が限定されることがあります．動詞のwalk は一般的に「歩く」の意味も「散歩する」の意味も表しますが，have a walk では「散歩する」の意味になります．また動詞によって意味が異なることもあります．have a drink は一般的に「アルコールを一杯飲む」の意味ですが，take a drink は飲み物の種類を限定せず「一杯飲む」の意味になります．それぞれの軽動詞と結びつく名詞には以下のようなものがあります．

Table 3.1.3　軽動詞の一覧

| | N に生じるもの |
|---|---|
| **give a N** | call, glimpse, indication, laugh, nod, shout, shrug, sigh, snort, speech, talk など |
| **make a N**<br>（主語の行為） | call, comeback, comment, effort, phone call, plan, purchase, try, turn, wish など |
| **take a N**（主語自身に益する行為が多い） | bite, drink, look, nap, ride, seat, sip, swim, trip, turn, walk など |
| **have a N** | dream, look, say, seat, sense など |

# 7　状態と動作

　be 動詞 + 名詞が動作を表すときには進行形や命令形になるときもあります．baby, coward, fool, idiot, jerk のような行為を非難する意味の名詞が多く使われます．

(51) He's **being** *a nuisance* again.

(52) She was worried about me. Also, she thought I **was being** *a fool*.

(53) I realized I **was being** *an idiot*.

(54) Don't **be** *a jerk*.

# 8　複数形の用法

複数名詞の用法には，以下のようなものがあります．

(55) 相互複数 (reciprocal plural)
 a. *Shaking hands* is now becoming popular in our country.
 b. Try to *make friends* with them.
 「列車を乗り換える」「握手をする」「友達になる」といった行為は2つの物を必要とするので目的語が複数になります．

(56) 配分複数 (distributive plural)
 Six people lost *their lives* in the accident.

人の命はひとりにひとつのものです．しかし複数の人が命を落とした場合，この例のように life は複数になります．複数の人がそれぞれ持っているひとつのもの（名詞）に対して同じ行為を行う場合に，その名詞が複数になることを配分複数と言います．次の例では，1人の子供がレインコートを1つずつ持ってくるのであって，1人の子供が複数のレインコートを持ってくるのではありません．

Tell the kids to bring *raincoats* to school tomorrow.

### ＜もっと詳しく＞　☞『現代高等英文法』p. 254
「「手を挙げる」は raise your hand か raise your hands か」

(57) 常時複数 (plurale tantum (plural only))
 常に複数形で使われる名詞を常時複数名詞と言います．この場合は，形が複数形ということであって，数の扱いは単数になる場合と複数に

なる場合があります．常時複数は，ペア名詞，複数形のみの名詞，不定複数があります．

　物がふたつの部分から成り全体で1組と考えられるような，glasses（眼鏡），scissors（ハサミ），jeans（ジーンズ）などをペア名詞と言います．これらは a pair of glasses のように a pair of をつけて数えます．a pair of glasses のようなときは単数扱いですが，two pairs of glasses や単に glasses の時は複数扱いです．このようなペア名詞には，chopsticks, dumbbells, earrings, jeans, glasses, gloves, pliers, scissors, shoes, sneakers, socks, stockings, sunglasses, tweezers などがあります．

　また -s で終わる学問名，病名は，形は複数形ですが，数の扱いは単数です．その例に aesthetics, economics, genetics, linguistics, mathematics, statistics や diabetes, herpes, hepatitis, measles, mumps などがあります．-s で終わる単語でも指示対象が単数の場合は単数扱い，複数の場合は複数扱いするものには，barracks, golf-links, headquarters, kennels, means, species などがあります．

　単数形と複数形で異なる意味を表すものがあります．例えば custom は「習慣」ですが customs は「税関」です．このような -s のついた形は常に複数扱いされます．arms, bearings, customs, forces, letters, looks などがその例です．

　数量が多いことを示す不定複数（indefinite plural）は常に複数扱いされます．apologies, bowels, congratulations, earnings, guts, pains, regards, savings, thanks, wages などがその例です．

(58)　総称複数（generic plural）

　名詞が表す種全体に当てはまることを述べるのは，総称（generic expression）と言います．総称は a＋単数名詞，the＋単数名詞といった表現でも表すことができますが，冠詞をつけない複数名詞でも表せます．

a.　*Tigers* and *lions* are quite similar anatomically and can be interbred.

b.　*Fresh figs* are generally available July through September.

　総称は「A は B だ」というその種全体に当てはまることを言うので，総称用法の名詞は主語に現れることがほとんどですが，場合によっては I like dogs. のように目的語に現れることもあります．Nora has been studying the medieval mystery play.／The best way to learn a language is to live among its speakers. のような the＋単数名詞，a＋単数名詞の総称の場合もあります．

---

### ！注意！

次の 3 つの総称の意味の違いを意識しましょう．
*Tigers* can be dangerous.（種の構成員全体を指して）
*A tiger* can be dangerous.（種の個々の成員を指して）
*The tiger* can be dangerous.（一般的性質を述べて）

---

## 9　主語と動詞の数の呼応

　数の一致については絶対的に決まっていると考えるよりは，単数扱いが多いとか複数扱いが多いとかいう傾向としてとらえるほうが現実に近いと言えます．

(59)　下線部の主語の文法的数に二重下線部の動詞が一致する場合

　　a.　The bat together with the balls was stolen.

　　b.　John, who was the chairman of the committee, as well as all the other members, was angry about the proposal of the government.

　　c.　You and I are free to trade with each other.

このような例では主語の文法的数に動詞の数も一致します．A or B や neither A nor B などでは動詞に近い B の数に呼応することもありますし，主語の A と B を結合していると考えて複数扱いになるときもあります．

(60)　A of B の形が主語になる場合

　　　　a.　A number of students were taking notes in the exhibition hall.

b. The number of students is expected to rise to 4,396 in 2008 from 2,866 in 1990.

c. A body of volunteers has been organized to aid the helpless in their struggle for survival.

d. None of us is / are perfect.

e. Neither of us is / are happy.

　A of B の形は，A と B のどちらが主語の名詞句の中心になるかによって数が決まります．A number of は配分詞ですので，中心は B の students でこちらが数を決定しますが，the number of の場合は，「…の数」が主語になるので，number に動詞の数が呼応します．none of や neither of の場合は単数・複数両方の扱いがあります．

(61)　主語の意味に一致する場合

a. Three years is a long time to wait.

b. Three years have passed since I came to Arizona.

c. Half of the students are from overseas.

d. Half of the apple was enough for me.

　数は，意味によって決まる場合があります．(61a) のように three years をひとつの期間としてひとまとまりに考えれば単数扱いですが，(61b) のように1年，2年と数えて時の経過が意識されるときは複数扱いになります．half of も後続する名詞によって，(61c) のように集団の構成員を言う場合は複数扱いですが，(61d) のように1つの固まりの部分を言う場合は単数扱いです．

　「1年半」を One year and a half というか One and a half years と言うかでも数の扱い方が異なります．前者の場合は One year and a half *has* passed. となりますが，後者の場合は years の複数の意識に引かれて One and a half years *have* passed. になる傾向にあります．

(62)　there 構文の数の一致

a. Is *there* any milk left?

b. *There* are a few things we need to discuss.

　c.　*There* is a barber shop, two Japanese restaurants and several used book stores in the mall.

　d.　*There*'s lives at stake and we can't afford to take any risks.

　there 構文の数は，be 動詞に後続する主語名詞の数によって決まります．一方，複数の主語であっても be 動詞に近い名詞に引かれて単数 is が用いられることもあります．また口語や非標準的な用法では，縮約形の there's がフレーズ化し名詞の数に関係なく使われることがあります．

# 10　冠詞

　英語の冠詞には，不定冠詞と定冠詞があります．不定冠詞は a / an，定冠詞は the です．英語の可算普通名詞は，文中では①不定冠詞を伴う（a president），②無冠詞で複数になる（presidents），③定冠詞を伴って単数・複数になる（the president(s)）のいずれかの形で使用されます．また，時に④無冠詞単数（president）になることがあります．④で使う場合は文法的・慣用的な理由があります．本書では，冠詞に，不定冠詞，定冠詞，無冠詞の 3 種類があると考え，それぞれを以下で説明していきます．

Table 3.1.4　冠詞の種類

| 不定冠詞 | a president |
|---|---|
| 定冠詞 | the president(s) |
| 無冠詞 | presidents |
| | president |

## 10.1　不定冠詞

　不定冠詞の用法には以下のようなものがあります．

Table 3.1.5　不定冠詞の用法

| 特定・不特定を表す | (1) We've got *a church* in a beautiful location on a quiet country. 〔特定〕<br>(2) They are going to build *a church* at the corner.　〔不特定〕 |
|---|---|
| 総称を表す | (3) *A child* needs love. |
| 種類・性質を表す | (4) I am *a Buddhist*.<br>(5) I believe him to be *a hard worker*.<br>(6) I had *a heavy breakfast* this morning; I am not hungry, thank you. |
| 数量・単位を表す | (7) A computer can store *a vast amount* of information.<br>(8) Gas costs ten dollars *a gallon* in western Europe. |
| a＋固有名詞 | (9) He is *a Shakespeare* of our time. |

　まず，(1)(2) を見てください．不定冠詞は，すでに具体的に存在している物や事に言及する特定的 (specific) な用法と，まだ存在していない不特定的 (non-specific) なものを表す用法を持っています．上の (1) の場合，すでにこの世に存在している教会を念頭に置いて a church と言っていますので特定的です．(2) の場合は，これから建てるまだ存在しない教会を示しています．この特定・不特定の区別により，共起する動詞の傾向が異なったりすることがありますので，意識しておくといいでしょう．すでに存在している教会には attend, join, visit, enter, destroy, rob, remodel, spot など，存在している物に対して行う行為を表す動詞が使われる傾向にあります．一方，(2) のような不特定の場合は build, construct, erect, establish, found などこれから作り出すことを意味する動詞と使われる傾向にあります．

　(3) は総称用法と言われるものです．名詞で表されている種に当てはめることができるような事態を述べるのに使います．例で示されているように，一般的に子供は1人ひとり愛情を必要とします．犬という種に属する動物がよいペットになるのも一般的なことですので，総称用法を使用し A dog makes a good pet. と言えます．

　次に (4) や (5) に示したように，不定冠詞を伴った可算名詞は，第 II 文型の

補語（S V C の C）や第 V 文型の目的格補語（S V O C の C）になって種類や性質を表します．不可算名詞に形容詞がついて，ある種類を表すようになると不定冠詞が使われます．

　例文（6）は不定冠詞が不可算名詞とともに使われて種類，個々の行為を表す例です．breakfast は通常は不可算名詞ですので，「朝食を食べる」は冠詞をつけず have breakfast と言いますが，（6）の I had a heavy breakfast this morning. のように，どんな朝食だったかを言う場合には不定冠詞がつきます．また，He told me this in San Francisco over a breakfast. のように個々の行為となるような場合も不定冠詞がつきます．

　例文（7）を見てください．a lot of / a bit of / a few of / a little of / a handful of / a large amount of / a large number of のように数量を言う名詞は a を伴います．また，例文（8）のように「…につき」という表現は単位を表しています．

　例文（9）のように，固有名詞に a がついた場合は，「…のような人，…という名前の人」の意味を表します．また，固有名詞が歴史上有名な場合，その属性に注目した普通名詞になっている場合もあります．a Judas（裏切者），a Hitler（独裁者），a Tsar（独裁者），a Rubicon（重大な分かれ目）などです．

## ＜もっと詳しく＞　☞『現代高等英文法』p. 284
「many a＋単数名詞 / a great many＋複数名詞の表現」

## 10.2　定冠詞

　定冠詞の用法には以下のようなものがあります．

Table 3.1.6　定冠詞の用法

| 歴史的・文化的に了解されている指示対象を指す | (1) *The earth* goes round *the sun*, and *the moon*, *the earth*. (地球は太陽の周りを，月は地球の周りをまわる) |
| --- | --- |
| 文脈・状況から了解されている指示対象を指す | (2) I saw a dog barking at the old man. *The dog* was a Doberman pincher, I guess. ［文脈］<br>(3) *The man* in a blue shirt is Jonnie. ［状況］<br>(4) Where is *the restroom?* ［状況］ |
| 順序によって了解されている指示対象を指す | (5) Monday is usually regarded as *the first day* of the week. |
| 総称を表す | (6) *The tiger* is in danger of extinction.<br>(7) *The Japanese* are a peace-loving people who want to avoid war.<br>(8) These seats are especially reserved for *the old* and *the handicapped*. |

　定冠詞は，話し手と聞き手にとって指示対象が了解できている場合に使われます．「the＋名詞句」の形を定名詞句 (definite noun phrase) と呼びます．定名詞句を使うための，話し手と聞き手の間の了解は，さまざまな条件で起こります．

　例文 (1) を見てください．話し手と聞き手が何を指しているかという了解が，歴史的・文化的な知識から生じる例です．the earth, the moon, the sun は持っている知識から唯一的に決定できるのは明解で，話し手と聞き手の了解ができています．このような名詞はほかにも the Pacific Ocean, the Hague, the University of Columbia, the Beatles などがあります．

　何を指しているかという了解は，文脈や状況から生まれることもあります．それを示したのが例文 (2) (3) (4) です．例文 (2) は，文脈で話題になった犬 (a dog) を，後で the dog で受ける場合で，文脈で了解が成立します．(3) では，何人か人がいる中で青いシャツを着た人が限定でき，状況から誰を指しているか明らかであれば，初めて話題に出てくる人でも the man in a blue shirt で表現します．(4) では，restroom は初めて話題として登場しても，学校や公園といった状況でトイレはあるものという前提があります．このような了解がありますので，初めて話題にしても the restroom となります．

　例文 (5) を見てみましょう．一番目，二番目…最後という順番は唯一的に決まりますので，She is the second of nine children. と定冠詞がつきます．このような順番を表す表現には the fist ～，the second ～，the last ～ や the next ～ などがあります．例えば the next station も今いる駅から次の駅というのは唯一的に決まりますので，the がつきます．気をつけなければならないのは，序数詞は序数とそれ以外の意味を表す場合があることです．例えば，second は「二番目」の意味と「ふたつめ，2度目」の意味を持っていますが，後者の意味では順番を限定しませんので不定冠詞を取ります．The bookcase needs a second coat of paint. (本棚はもう一回ペンキを塗る必要がある) / Please Captain, give me a second chance. (もう一度チャンスをください) などの例がそれを示しています．

　例文 (6) (7) (8) で示すように，「the＋単数名詞」は総称を表すこともあります．国籍や民族名に the をつけて総称を表すこともあります．「the＋形容詞」もある種の総称で，社会の中である属性を持った人たちの集団を指します．よく使われるものは以下のようなものです．the rich / the poor / the young / the middle-aged / the old / the strong / the hungry / the privileged / the underprivileged / the unemployed / the sick / the dead などです．

## ＜もっと詳しく＞　☞『現代高等英文法』p. 287
「the＋形容詞が一人の人を指す場合や抽象的意味を表す場合」


## 10.3　無冠詞

　一般的に可算単数名詞はその名詞が表すものを指しますが，一方でその名詞が表すものの性質・機能・用途などの観点から，そのものを抽象的にとらえることができます．その場合，「無冠詞＋単数名詞」になります．また，音調の理由や，文頭に来ている場合にも無冠詞になることがあります．下に挙げる例で一つひとつ確認しましょう．

Table 3.1.7　無冠詞の用法

| 抽象化する場合 | (1) How often do you **go to** *church*?<br>(2) Most Americans commute **by** *car*.<br>(3) George W. Bush was **elected** *president* of the United States in 2000.<br>(4) I have two **kinds of** *signature*. I use them differently. |
|---|---|
| 形容詞化する場合 | (5) Are you *man* enough for the job?<br>(6) That animal is only partly *dog*. |
| 省略・脱落する場合 | (7) The whole thing has been a fiasco **from** *start* **to** *finish*.　[省略]<br>(8) *Fact* is, China is feverishly building its own machinery industry.　[脱落]<br>(9) Fourteen houses were raided and 52 people were **taken** *prisoner* that night.　[省略] |
| 掛け声・新聞の見出し・掲示・呼びかけなどで使用する場合 | (10) Insert a plug in *hole* in *side panel*.　[説明書などでの説明]<br>(11) *Fire*!　[掛け声]<br>(12) *Huge snowstorm* heads for *US east coast*.　[見出し] |

　例文（1）を見てみましょう．go to bed／study in class／appear in court／go to prison／go to school／go to town／go to university／go to work のように名詞の表すものの機能や役割だけに注目する場合に，冠詞が省略されます．「学校」「病院」などは習慣的に利用する場所の機能（勉強する，病気を治す）が皆に理解されているからです．また（2）に挙げたように，習慣的に利用する乗り物を表すby train／by bus／by air／by boat なども同じ理屈です．一方で，by で導かれていても習慣的でない場合は冠詞がつきます．例えば The crew were retrieved *by a helicopter* and taken to the recovery ship.／She was hit and killed *by a car*. と比較してみましょう．

　また（3）で示すように，名詞の表す人が担う唯一的な役職を表す場合も抽象化しているので無冠詞です．ここでは「ひとりひとりの大統領」を指すのではなく，「大統領という役職」の意味になります．

　（4）のように，kind of なども種類を言うために後続する名詞は抽象化され，無冠詞で単数名詞が来るのがふつうです（口語では What kind of a car …? となる場合もあります．複数は those kinds of book か those kinds of books となります）．

　（5）のように，man を「一人の男」ではなく「男らしい」という意味で使うことがあります．この場合形容詞化しており enough を伴って用いられることがあります．ただ現在の社会ではこのような表現は時代に合わないので注意しましょう．He's only about a third teacher and the rest of him is tyrant.（（彼の性格を述べて）あいつは3分の1が教師で残りは独裁者だ）のような特殊な例も見られます．（6）は「その動物はほんの一部だけが犬に過ぎない」の意味で，もともと名詞であった dog が形容詞化し無冠詞で使われています．

　（7）は，from A to B のような対比を表す表現や対になるような表現で無冠詞となった例です．このような対比や対を表す表現には，from mouth to mouth / from hand to mouth / hand in hand / camera in hand / foot in mouth / year after year / day by day / year on year などがあります．（8）は文頭に来て冠詞が脱落した例です．この種の例はそう多くありません．（9）は，be taken prisoner という形で成句化したものです．

　（10）（11）（12）のように，新聞の見出しや掛け声，呼びかけでは無冠詞になります．

### ＜もっと詳しく＞　☞『現代高等英文法』p. 290

「A Happy New Year! とは言わず，Happy New Year! と言う」
「have (the) flu の英米での違い」

# ◉練習問題◉

1　次の文のかっこの中に，a/an, the，無冠詞（冠詞なし）のどれかを入れなさい．

Actors Gen Hoshino and Yui Aragaki played unusual, but appealing, lovers in （　1　） well-liked Japanese TV show. Now, they are really getting married. （　2　） couple announced their decision in （　3　） joint statement posted Wednesday on Aragaki's Instagram account. It is （　4　） example of "life imitates art," which means that life sometimes seems to be a copy of a work of （　5　） art. That is amusing because we usually think of art as a copy of something in real life. "We would like to announce that we, （　6　） Gen Hoshino and （　7　） Yui Aragaki, are getting married," （　8　） statement said. "We hope you will continue to warmly support us both." Aragaki and Hoshino acted together in （　9　） 2016 humorous show, "Nigeru wa Haji da ga Yaku ni Tatsu," or "It's Shameful to Run, but It Works." Hoshino played （　10　） businessman who hires （　11　） young woman, played by Aragaki, as a housekeeper. They begin with （　12　） business relationship. They slowly develop （　13　） feelings of love for each other. They decide on an agreement that is a little like marriage, but only for three years. （　14　） story spoke to one problem in （　15　） Japanese society: young people are waiting until later in （　16　） life to marry and have children. The result is one of the lowest birth rates in （　17　） world.　　　　(Voice of America, May 20, 2021)

2　Oral translation: （　　　）内の語句を使用して，以下の日本文を英語にしなさい．

2.1　昨日大阪で靴を 2 足買った．

_____

2.2　彼は 1 週間以上インフルエンザで寝こんでいる．

_____

2.3　5 年は技術の世界では長いよ．

_____

2.4   お茶をもう一杯いかがですか.

2.5   私のペットはどっちがいいでしょう，猫かな，犬かな. (Which kind of pet … )

2.6   私の望みは社会に奉仕することです.

2.7   私の理解では，この携帯電話には 3 年間の保証がついていると思います. (it is my understanding that / there is / three-year warranty)

2.8   お好み焼きを作るには，小麦粉，水，薄く切った豚肉数枚，千切りしたキャベツ，卵が必要です.

2.9   今朝はサラダ食べた？　顔にトマトがついてるよ.

2.10 新しいことや考えを受け入れるのがいいと思うよ (My advice is … / open your mind for … )

2.11 彼は大家族で，彼は 5 人きょうだいの上から 2 番目だそうだ. (his family … )

# 第2章　代名詞

（『現代高等英文法』pp. 262 〜 279 に該当）

## 1　代名詞

代名詞（pronoun）は，名詞（句）の代用をします．前後の名詞（句）だけでなく，文脈や状況で明らかな事柄を指したり，漠然と状況を指したりします．英語の代名詞には，人称代名詞，指示代名詞，不定代名詞，疑問代名詞，関係代名詞があります（疑問代名詞と関係代名詞は PART III 第6章で扱います）．

(1) *I*'ve known the Browns for a long time. *They*'re very pleasant people.　[人称代名詞]

(2) *Those* look riper than these.　[指示代名詞]

(3) *One* cannot always be right, can *one*?　[不定代名詞]

(4) *Who* is that woman?　[疑問代名詞]

(5) Do you know the people *who* live over the road?　[関係代名詞]

## 2　人称代名詞

人称代名詞は，人称と数に応じて次の表のように変化します．

Table 3.2.1   人称代名詞の変化

| 人称 | 数 | 主格 | 所有格 | 目的格 | 所有代名詞 |
|---|---|---|---|---|---|
| 1 人称 | 単数 | I | my | me | mine |
| 2 人称 | | you | your | you | yours |
| 3 人称 | | he, she, it | his, her, its | him, her, it | his, hers, -- |
| 1 人称 | 複数 | we | our | us | ours |
| 2 人称 | | you | your | you | yours |
| 3 人称 | | they | their | them | theirs |

　主格は主語に，目的格は動詞・前置詞の目的語に，所有格は名詞の前に使われます．主語であっても Jack and *me* are going skiing this weekend. のように原則から外れる例もあります．Who said that? という疑問文に，*Her.* や It was *her.* と答えることもあります．

　所有代名詞 (possessive pronoun) は，所有格 + 名詞の代用をします．This is my book, and that's yours. の yours は your book の代用です．現代英語では，it の所有代名詞はなく，代わりに its own といった形で表現することがあります．I agree that science has its scope of operation and faith has its own. のようなものがその例です．

　所有格は冠詞や指示代名詞と並列できませんので，「彼女のある本」「あなたのあの本」と表現するには a book of hers や that book of yours のように，「限定詞 + 名詞 + of + 所有代名詞」の形にします．


## 2.1  it の多様な用法

it は次のような多様な用法を持っています．

(6) a. *It's* ten o'clock.　　　　　　　　　　　　　[時の it, 非人称]

　　 b. *It* will be cloudy today.　　　　　　　　　　[天候の it, 非人称]

　　 c. How far is *it* to your farm?　　　　　　　　[距離の it, 非人称]

　　 d. *It* seems that he is ill.　　　　　　　　　　[非人称動詞の主語]

(7) a. *It* annoys me **to see him getting ahead of me**.　　　[仮主語]

　　 b. I consider *it* appropriate **to provide constructive criticism**.

　　　　　　　　　　　　　　　　　　　　　　　　　　[仮目的語]

　　 c. *It* amazed her **that he could be so calm at such a time**.　[仮主語]

　　 d. I think *it* necessary **that arrangements be made**.　　[仮目的語]

　　 e. *It*'s nice **meeting you**.　　　　　　　　　　　　　　[仮主語]

(8)　Everyone knows we cheated. *It* was obvious.　　　[文・節の代用]

(9)　*It*'s terrible—everybody's got colds, and the central heating isn't working.　　　　　　　　　　　　　　　　　　　　　　[状況]

(10)　*It* is parents who should be supporting their own children.

　　　　　　　　　　　　　　　　　　　　　　　　　　[分裂文の主語]

(11)　I finally made *it* home and straight into Nick's arms.　　[虚辞の it]

(11) の it は何かを指しているわけではなく it に意味はありません．この it はフレーズの一部に現れ，フレーズ全体としてある意味を表します．例えば bus it to …, dish it out, get away from it, lord it over …, make it to …, sleep it off, step on it, take it up with …, walk it off, whoop it up などがあります．

## 2.2　総称の we, you, they, one

(12)　*We* can use cell phones to send text messages.

(13)　When *you*'re with him, he makes you feel very important.

(14)　*They* say it will be a mild weather.

(15)　*One* should always try to keep one's temper.

代名詞で総称を表す方法には，話し手を含んだ人一般を言う we（=(12)），聞き手を含んだ you（=(13)），話し手と聞き手を除いた人一般をさす they（=(14)）があります．また one（=(15)）は不定代名詞ですが，you と置き換えることのできる総称で堅苦しい言い方です．

## 2.3　単数を受ける they

everyone, anyone, each person は性別に関係なく使えます．これらは単数扱いですが，英語には性別を指定しない単数代名詞がありませんでした．かつては everyone などは he とその変化形で指すというのが文法の規則でした．しかし，そうすると「みんな」の中に女性などが含まれていないという意識も出てきます．そこでその役割を they とその変化形が担うようになりました．単数の they ですが，動詞は複数呼応します．

(16)　We should give everyone a chance to say what *they* think.

(17)　If anyone doesn't like it, *they* can leave.

(18)　Tell each person to help *themselves* to what they want.

また昨今の時代の要請を受けて，they が性別を指定しない単数代名詞として使われるようになりました．男性か女性かを指定せずに使える代名詞で「バイナリーの they」(binary *they*) と呼ばれます．I talked to one of my friends. *They* said ... のようなものです．本来ならば友人の性に応じて He said ... か She said ... となるところですが，They を使うことで性別を決めつけることなく代用できます．

## 2.4　人称代名詞の照応関係

代名詞が名詞句を受けることを照応 (reference) と言います．代名詞が前に出てきた名詞を受けると前方照応 (anaphoric reference)，代名詞が後に出てくる名詞を受けると後方照応 (cataphoric reference) と言います．以下の例で，代名詞はどういう環境でどの名詞を受けるのかを考えてみましょう．

(19)　a.　**John** loves *his* mother.

　　　　　　　　　　　　[his は John を指す場合と全く別の男性を指す場合がある]

　　　b.　*He* loves **John's** mother.　　　　[He は John ではない別の男性を指す]

　　　c.　**John's** mother loves *him*.

　　　　　　　　　　　　[him は John を指す場合と全く別の男性を指す場合がある]

　　　d.　*His* mother loves **John**.　　　　　[His は John ではない別の男性を指す]

(20)　a.　Near *him*, **Dan** saw a snake.

　　　　　　　　　　　　[him は Dan を指す場合と別の男性を指す場合がある]

　　　b.　**Dan** saw a snake near *him*.

　　　　　　　　　　　　[him は Dan を指す場合と別の男性を指す場合がある]

(21)　a.　**Masako** went to town after *she* woke up.

　　　　　　　　　　　　[she は Masako を指す場合と別の女性を指す場合がある]

　　　b.　After *she* woke up, **Masako** went to town.

　　　　　　　　　　　　[she は Masako ではない別の女性を指す]

(22)　a.　Near **Dan**, *he* saw a snake.　　　[he は Dan ではなく別の男性を指す]

　　　b.　After **Masako** woke up, *she* went to town.

　　　　　　　　　　　　[she は Masako ではない別の女性を指す]

(23)　a.　*She* thought **Ann** couldn't win.　[She は Ann ではない別の女性を指す]

　　　b.　**Ann** thought *she* couldn't win.

　　　　　　　　　　　　[she は Ann を指す場合と別の女性を指す場合がある]


## ＜もっと詳しく＞　　☞『**現代高等英文法**』p. 270

「人称代名詞の名詞化」


# 3　再帰代名詞

　再帰代名詞（reflexive pronoun）は -self 形を持ち，① Ｓ Ｖ Ｃ/Ｓ Ｖ Ｏ で Ｓ と C/O が同じ人・物を指す場合や Ｓ と前置詞の目的語が同じ人・物を指す場合 (24)，②行為を自ら行ったことを強調する場合 (25)，③ ①と②のような理由がなく，特に必然性のない場合 (26) に使われます．

　(24)　a.　Have **you** locked *yourself* out? [S = O] (I told **him** to help *himself*.
　　　　　　のようなものは Ｓ Ｖ Ｏ が tell の動詞型に入り込んだと考えますの

で，このタイプです.)

   b.  Most **authors** start by writing novels about *themselves*.

[S＝前置詞の目的語]

   c.  **He** is not *himself* today.  [S＝C]

(25)   The **headmaster** *himself* met us at the door./The **headmaster** met us at the door *himself.*

(26)   The boss asked John and *myself* to give a brief presentation.

ほかに be beside oneself with ... といったフレーズや enjoy oneself といった「他動詞＋oneself」で自動詞的な意味を表す表現に再帰代名詞が現れます.


# 4　指示代名詞

(27)   *This* is the book I've been looking for.

(28)   *These* are the days of the Beatles and Bob Dylan and so-called protest music.

(29)   *That* is the place I come from.

(30)   *Those* are the people we have to thank.

(31) a.  New York's poverty rate is higher than *that* of the rest of the US.

     b.  Trollope's novels are more entertaining than *those* of Dickens.

指示代名詞 (demonstrative pronoun) は，単数の this, that，複数の these, those があります. this, these は物理的・心理的に話し手に近いもの，人，場所，時間などあらゆるものを指して使われます. that, those は物理的・心理的に話し手から遠いもの，人，場所，時間などあらゆるものを指して使われます. (31) のように that と those には同じ名詞の繰り返しを避ける用法があります.

**! 注意 !**

　(31) の場合，まとまりのある名詞句の中の一部の名詞を取り出して that や those に置き換えることはできません．The cup of coffee I had this morning was better than that I was served at the coffee shop. では the cup of coffee というまとまり全体を that で置き換えることはできますが，the cup だけを置き換えて × that of coffee とはできません．The number of people who speak Chinese is larger than the number of people speaking any other language. においても the number だけを that に置き換えることはできません（× that of people speaking any other language）．

## 5　不定代名詞

　不定代名詞（indefinite pronoun）は，「指示対象が指定されない代名詞」のことで，単純形と複合形があります．

Table 3.2.2　不定代名詞のいろいろ

| 単純形 | ①代名詞用法と名詞の前に置く限定詞用法を持つ | all, both; each; any, some; either, neither; other, another |
|---|---|---|
| | ②代名詞用法のみ | one, none |
| 複合形<br>（単純形①＋ **body / one / thing**） | | someone, somebody, something; anyone, anybody, anything; no one, nobody, nothing; every one, everybody, everything |

　単純形①に挙げたものは，単独でも使えます．また，名詞の前に置くこともできます．さらに of 句を後続させることもあります．数の扱いについては以下の用例で単数扱いされているか，複数扱いされているかを確認しましょう．

(32) a.  *All* that glitters is not gold.

　　 b.  *All* of us have to go.

(33) a.  *Both* arrived at the same time.

　　 b.  *Both* of the leaders expressed hope that the talks would continue.

(34) a.  We *each* ( = Every one of us) wanted the bedroom with the bal-
　　　　 cony, so tossed a coin to decide.

　　 b.  *Each* of the companies supports a local charity.

(35) a.  The children needed new school clothes and Kim couldn't afford
　　　　 *any*.

　　 b.  *Some* of us had different circumstances growing up.

(36) a.  There's tea or coffee—you can have *either*.

　　 b.  *Neither* of them can cook.

(37) a.  'Have you got a camera?' 'No.' 'You should buy *one*.'

　　 b.  *One* of the windows was open.

(38) a.  I thought there was some coffee in the cupboard, but there's *none*
　　　　 there.

　　 b.  *None* of my friends will help me.

(39) a.  He sat in front of the fire rubbing one bare foot against the *other*.

　　 b.  There'll never be *another* like him.

(40)　 *Everybody* in this street has a car.

(41)　 *Something* in the cupboard smells odd.


## 5.1　不定代名詞 one の用法

　不定代名詞の one は，①総称で不特定多数を表す場合，②前に出ている名詞
の同種別物を指す場合，③ a の代用をする限定詞の用法があります．

(42)　 *One* should always try to keep *one's* temper.　　　　　　[総称]

(43)　 Mummy, will you buy me a bus? I want that red *one*.　　[同種別物]

(44)　 I'd like a cup of coffee. —Pour yourself *one*.　　　　　　[限定詞]

総称の one をさらに代名詞で受ける場合は，one を繰り返したり，he or she
や they で受けたりします．

(45)　If there were nothing unusual to look forward to, *one* wouldn't want
　　　to get up early in the morning, would *one*?

(43) の one は，バスのおもちゃを指します．I have **a bus**. *It* is red. のよう
な場合は It は私が持っているバスのおもちゃそのものを指しますが，(43) の場
合は，同一物そのものを指すのではなく，同種のものを指しています．この one
には this や that がついたり，形容詞での修飾が可能です．複数形は ones とな
ります．
　一方，(44) の場合は，one (cup of coffee) のことであり，複数形は two /
three / four … と具体的な数字であったり some … であったりします．
　次の例は one と it の違いを明確に示しています．

(46)　They are going to build **a church** at the end of the street. *It* is going
　　　to be a second *one* in town.

a church はまだ存在しない教会ですが，その教会を指す場合は同一物を指示す
る it になります．それは町でふたつめの教会で，同種別物を言いますから one
となります．

## 5.2　不定代名詞 -thing / -one / -body の修飾

　複合形の不定代名詞は，形容詞や to 不定詞，関係節などで修飾が可能です．
通常は後に修飾語を置きます．また there 構文で使うこともできます．

(47)　And there's *nothing* interesting about my life to tell.
(48)　There were no signs of violence, *nothing* to suggest that his death
　　　had not been peaceful.
(49)　"There's *nobody* who can hold a candle to him," Mona added.
(50)　There's *someone* at the door.

時に an immensely powerful *something*（とてつもない力を持つ何か）のような，修飾語が前置する形が見られます．

## ◉練習問題◉

**1 かっこに適切な代名詞を入れなさい．日本語がある場合はそれを参考にしなさい．**

1.1  You can use reusable bags for gifts. Keep gift bags and other decorations that you receive. You can reuse (　　　　　) the next time you give a gift.

1.2  I would like to thank (　　　　　) of you for joining us today.
（皆さんお一人お一人に）

1.3  The headmaster explained the role of the Parent Teacher Association, (　　　　　) importance and procedure.

1.4  Climbing plants are also popular.  Social media sites show images of rooms filled with vines rooted in containers. (　　　　　) spread over furniture, doorways, and other things in the room.

1.5  (　　　　　) rosemary and bay laurel come from the part of the world near the Mediterranean Sea.（どちらも）

1.6  Unlike type 1 patients, (　　　　　) with type 2 diabetes may be able to manage or reduce the severity of their illness through diet and exercise.

1.7  That was the question that Mike could not bring (　　　　　) to ask.

1.8  John opened (　　　　　) mouth to respond, but (　　　　　) came out. He remained silent.

1.9  She lay in (　　　　　) bed surrounded by dolls and stuffed animals.
（彼女は自分のベッドに）

## 2　Oral translation: (　　) 内の語句を利用して，日本文を英語にしなさい.

2.1　赤い靴はいりません. あの黒いのを見せてください.

_____

2.2　友達ってお互いを信用するものだよ.

_____

2.3　僕には隠すことなどないよ. (nothing to …)

_____

2.4　私に何をしてほしいのですか.

_____

2.5　新しい研究によると，人間の子供の笑うパターンがほかの種のそれと似ているとのことだ. (A new study finds / the laughing patterns)

_____

2.6　母親が帰り道に私のことを待ってくれていました.

_____

2.7　こんなことが起こるなんて誰も思っていなかった. (None of us)

_____

2.8　コーヒーが好きな人たちの中には毎日自分が飲むコーヒーについてツイッターで何かつぶやいている人がいる. (coffee lovers / tweet)

_____

2.9　彼は人生の半分以上をニューヨークで過ごして，それは幸せに満ちたものでした. (more than half of his life)

_____

2.10　彼女が立ち上げたような事業を僕が立ち上げるのは簡単ではない.
(build / that sort of business)

_____

# 第3章　形容詞と限定詞

（『現代高等英文法』pp. 291 〜 327 に該当）

## 1　形容詞の概観

　形容詞は，「名詞の意味を限定したり，名詞に関して叙述する働きをしたりする語（句）」と定義します．

### 1.1　種類

　上記の定義に基づくと，形容詞は次の 7 種類に分類されます．

① 性質形容詞 (quality adjective,

　　例：Their mother was a very *beautiful* woman.)

② 指示形容詞 (demonstrative adjective, *this, that, these, those,*

　　例：How big are *those* craters on the Moon?)

③ 配分詞 (distributive, *each, every, either, neither,*

　　例：*Each* factor is not mutually exclusive.)

④ 数量詞 (quantifier, *some, any, no, little, few, many, much, one,*

　　例：I don't have *much* money with me.)

⑤ 疑問形容詞 (interrogative adjective, *which, what, whose,*

　　例：*Whose* book is this?)

⑥ 関係形容詞 (relative adjective, *whose, which, what,*

　　例：He has lost *what* little respect many people had for him.)

⑦ 人称代名詞の所有格 (*my, your, his, her, its, our, their,*

　　例：This is *my* book, and that's yours.)

　本章は，もっとも普通に形容詞と呼ばれる①の性質形容詞を中心に扱います．
②，③，④はまとめて限定詞として説明します．⑤と⑥は PART III 第 6 章，⑦
は，PART III 第 2 章を参照してください．


## 1.2　機能・特徴・語順

　これまでの研究によると，形容詞は (1) に示す特徴を持ちます．(1a, b) は形
容詞の機能であり，(1c, d) は形容詞の性質を表しています．すべての形容詞が，
(1) の 4 つの特徴を持つわけではありませんが，どのような形容詞であるかを判
断する上で重要な特徴となります．

(1) a.　名詞の限定修飾機能 (attributive function) を持つ.

　　　　例：We saw a *beautiful* sunset as we drove.

　　b.　主格補語・目的格補語として叙述機能 (predicative function) を持
　　　　つ.

　　　　例：He was *hard-working* and *honest*.

　　c.　強意副詞 (intensifier) の very で修飾できる.

　　　　例：The fishing industry is *very important* to the area.

　　d.　比較級 (comparative)・最上級 (superlative) の比較変化を持つ.

　　　　例：I think things are going from *bad* to *worse* in the town.

　(1a, b) は，次節で説明する限定用法か叙述用法の違いを説明しています．
(1c) は，本章 2.3 節で説明する段階性 (gradable) に関係します．(1) 以外に，
形容詞の重要な特徴があります．それについては，次節以降で説明します．
　形容詞は，Table 3.3.1 に示す語順で使用される傾向にあります．注意をして
ほしいのは，Table 3.3.1 に示すすべての要素が必要，というわけではありませ
ん．(2) を参照してください．

Table 3.3.1　形容詞の語順

| 冠詞・限定詞 | 形容詞 | | | | | | 名詞 (句) |
|---|---|---|---|---|---|---|---|
| | 評価 | サイズ | 新古 | 色彩 | 所属 | 材料 | |
| a, the, my, this など | pretty beautiful nice | little big | young old new | white orange | Japanese Victorian | stone | children house open car |

(2) a.　They are *pretty little young Japanese* children.

[評価　サイズ　新古　所属]

　　b.　They live in *a big beautiful old white Victorian stone* house.

[サイズ 評価　新古 色彩　所属　材料]

　　c.　We have *a nice big new orange open* car.

[評価　サイズ　新古　色彩　複合語の一部]


## 2　限定用法と叙述用法

　形容詞は，名詞の前に来て意味を限定する限定用法（attributive use）と be 動詞などの後にきて補語の役割をする叙述用法（predicative use）を持ちます．(3) が限定用法の例で，(4) が叙述用法の例となります．

(3) a.　The *main* reason we lost the game was that we had never played in front of so many people before.

　　b.　A guy talked to me on the street, but I found he was a *total* stranger.

(4) a.　The baby was *asleep* in the crib.

　　b.　Our boat was *adrift* on the ocean for five days.

　(3) の形容詞 main と total は，限定用法でのみ使用されます．(4) の asleep と adrift は叙述用法のみで使用されます．多くの形容詞は，I saw a *tall* girl./ The girl is *tall.* の tall のように限定用法と叙述用法の両方を持ちます．

　限定用法，叙述用法のどちらで使用されるのかを判断する方法として，①それぞれの形容詞をリストする方法，②恒常的・一時的の意味に違いを求める方法，③段階的・非段階的の意味に違いを求める方法，の3つがこれまでの研究で提唱されました．この判断方法に頼らなくとも，限定用法か叙述用法，もしくは両方の用法を持つのかを知りたい場合は，学習者用英和辞典を引いてください．そうすると，調べた形容詞が，どのような用法を持つのかが書かれています．

　形容詞句には，「前置詞＋（形容詞）＋名詞」からなるものも含まれます．例えば，of great importance, of no use などのように叙述用法で使われるフレーズです．限定用法の形容詞句は，場所を表す前置詞＋名詞（My friends *in Hawaii* are all Samoans.）のようなものがあります．

## ＜もっと詳しく＞　☞『**現代高等英文法**』p. 295f.
「(1) 限定用法と名詞前置用法」，「(2) a recent acquaintance と ×a recent friend」

## 3　段階性

以下の例文を見てください．

(5) a.　How famous is she?—She is *very* famous.
　　b.　×How dead is he?—×He is *very* dead.

(5a) の famous はどの程度有名であるかを問い，答えることが可能ですが，(5b) の dead はどの程度死んでいるかを問い，答えることはできません．つまり，famous は段階性がありますが，dead は段階性がありません．この段階性をもつ形容詞を修飾するものとして，very があります．

　段階性を持たない形容詞として，国民を表す Japanese, American, Canadian, 名詞由来の alphabetical, atomic, choral, criminal, federal 等，極限を表す absolute, complete, correct, dead, equal, essential, impossible, infinite, total, unique などがあります．このような形容詞は，程度を表すことがないため，比較変化を

せず，very などの強意語で修飾されることはありません．ただし，語義によっ
ては段階性を持つ場合があります（例：This *very* **British** comedy is about a
series of outrageous frauds. この British は「イギリスの」ではなくて，「イギリ
ス的な」の意味）.

## ＜もっと詳しく＞　☞『**現代高等英文法**』p. 298
「非段階形容詞の delicious」


## 4　一時性もしくは永続性

　形容詞には，進行形や命令形にできる，ある行為を行った時に見られる性質や
状態を表す一時性形容詞（temporary adjective）と，進行形や命令形にできない，
本来的に備わった性質をいう永続性形容詞（permanent adjective）があります.
　前者を（6）に示します．進行形・命令形の部分は太字表記，形容詞はイタリッ
ク表記としています．（6）以外の一時性形容詞をいくつか（7）に列挙します.
（7）に提示した形容詞は，永続性形容詞として使用されないというわけではな
い，ということに注意してください.

(6) a.　**Don't** be *silly*!
　　b.　**Be** *careful*!
　　c.　(**Be**) *Quiet*, please!
　　d.　It's great that you **are being** *honest* with yourself.
　　e.　I realized I **was being** *unfair* to you.
(7)　angry, brave, careful, careless, caution, dull, fair, faithful, foolish,
　　frank, friendly, funny, generous, good, greedy, haste, honest, insis-
　　tent, jealous, kind, nice, noisy, patient, pleasant, quiet, rude, sensible,
　　silly, slow, stupid, thoughtful, unfair, unpleasant, wise など

次に永続性形容詞を（8）にあげます.

(8)　alive, beautiful, cold, dead, delicious, fragrant, heavy, high, honest, hot, intelligent, light, long, old, precious, pretty, ripe, short, soft, sour, smart, sweet, tall, tasty, tender, ugly, young など

(7) と (8) の両方にリストされている形容詞に honest があります．honest は，一時的に「正直になる，正直に話す」という意味を持つ形容詞で使用されますが，I like people who are *honest* and principled and who care about others. というように人が永続的に持っている性質を言う場合もあります．

　一時性及び永続性の両方で使用される形容詞もあれば，永続性形容詞から一時性形容詞へ変化する形容詞もあります．本来 beautiful は永続性形容詞ですが，(9) の beautiful は一時的な意味で使用されています．その場合，beautiful は enough to, so ~ that の構文で使用されます．

(9) a.　She is *beautiful* enough to turn men's heads.
　　 b.　The garden was so *beautiful* that she began to like it more than anything else.

形容詞が永続的な意味で使用される場合と，一時性の意味で使用される場合では，次節で説明する形容詞型（ある形容詞が特徴的に使用される統語形式）が異なります．


# 5　形容詞型

　一時性形容詞は，意味によって独自の型（＝統語形式）をとります．(10) に示す 5 つの形容詞型 (adjective pattern) が基本となります．Adj. = Adjective（形容詞），NP = Nouns Phrase（名詞句），that = that 節，to do = to 不定詞，PrepP. = Prepositional Phrase（前置詞句）を意味します．

## ＜もっと詳しく＞　☞『**現代高等英文法**』p. 302
「個々の形容詞と形容詞型」

(10) a.　[It is Adj. that]　　　It is *important* that he attended every day.

　　b.　[NP be Adj. that]　　I am *happy* that I could come.

　　c.　[It is Adj. to do]　　It is *dangerous* for him *to swim* across the river.

　　d.　[NP is Adj. to do]　　I'm *glad to see* you.

　　e.　[NP is Adj. PrepP]　　I am very *anxious* **about** the health of the President.

それぞれの形容詞型の特徴をまとめたものが，Table 3.3.2 となります．

Table 3.3.2　形容詞型の特徴

| 形容詞型 | 形容詞の種類 | 形容詞の例とその他の特徴 |
|---|---|---|
| It is Adj. that | (1) モダリティ | (1) acceptable, apparent, clear, cool, fine, fortunate, interesting, nice, well-known など |
| | (2) 指示 | (2) advisable, certain, important, urgent, vital など |
| | (3) 不確定な予測 | (3) conceivable, doubtful, imaginable, likely など, that 節には法助動詞が使用されることがある |
| | (4) 信念 | (4) certain, correct, definite, plausible, true など, 否定文もしくは不確定の場合は wh 節が使用される傾向 |
| NP be Adj. that | (1) 感情 | (1) amazed, angry, astonished, happy, pleased など. that 節の代わりに感情が生じる理由を言う because 節が使用されることもある |
| | (2) 確信・認識 | (2) aware, certain, confident, determined, sure など, wh 節をとることがある |
| | (3) 主張 | (3) categorical, definite, emphatic, firm, insistent など |
| | (4) 葛藤 | (4) afraid, anxious, careful, desperate, eager など. that 節には法助動詞が使用されることがある |

| It is Adj. to do | (1) 行動評価 | (1) accurate, dangerous, natural, unfair, wrong など. It is Adj. that 節で使用されることもある |
| | (2) 人・事物の評価 | (2) awkward, boring, brilliant, cheap, safe など. NP is Adj. to do に書き換え可能 |
| | (3) 行為に基づく人の評価 | (3) bold, brave, kind, nasty, selfish, shameless など. It is Adj. of ... to do で使用されることもある |
| NP is Adj. to do | (1) 人・事物の評価 | (1) awkward, boring, brilliant, cheap, clever, foolish, safe など. It is Adj. to do に書き換え可能 |
| | (2) 感情 | (2) amused, angry, delighted, displeased, upset など |
| | (3) 行動の速度 | (3) quick, slow, soft, to 不定詞で行動を表す |
| | (4) be Adj. to が準擬似法助動詞 | (4) be anxious to, be eager to, be inadequate to, be certain to など |
| NP is Adj. PrepP | | 「形容詞＋前置詞句」で使用される. be anxious about, be good at, be certain of, be interested in など |

## ＜もっと詳しく＞　☞『**現代高等英文法**』p. 304

「(1) It would be nice if という異形」,「(2) it is surprising how / what ... : it は間接感嘆文の代理」,「(3) it is (just) as well (that) という成句」

## ＜もっと詳しく＞　☞『**現代高等英文法**』p. 312

「It is silly of you to do と It is silly for you to do」

## 6　限定詞

限定詞（determiner）は，名詞の前にきて，その名詞の数量の多少，所有関係などを示す形容詞的な働きをする語句のことです．（11a〜g）の種類があります．

(11) a.　冠詞：a, an, the

　　 b.　部分詞：some, any, many, much, a cup of, a large number of など

　　 c.　数量語：one, two など

　　 d.　指示形容詞：this, that など

　　 e.　所有名詞：John's など

　　 f.　配分詞：each, every など

　　 g.　人称代名詞の所有格：my, his など

限定詞は，限定する対象が可算名詞か不可算名詞か，また肯定文か否定・疑問文かで役割が異なります．その一覧が Table 3.3.3 です．

Table 3.3.3　限定詞の一覧

| 限定詞 | 可算名詞 | | 不可算名詞 | | 代名詞用法 | 副詞用法 | 用例 |
|---|---|---|---|---|---|---|---|
| | 肯定文 | 否定文・疑問文 | 肯定文 | 否定文・疑問文 | | | |
| all | ✔ | ✔ | ✔ | ✔ | ✔ | ✔ | (12) |
| every | ✔ | ✔ | | | | | (13a) |
| each | ✔ | ✔ | | | ✔ | | (13b) |
| many | ✔ | ✔ | | | ✔ | | (14) |
| much | | | ✔ | ✔ | ✔ | ✔ | (14) |
| some | ✔ | ✔ | ✔ | ✔ | ✔ | ✔ | (15) |
| any | ✔ | ✔ | ✔ | ✔ | ✔ | ✔ | (15) |
| (a) few | ✔ | | | | ✔ | | (16) |
| (a) little | | | ✔ | | ✔ | ✔ | (17) |
| no | ✔ | | ✔ | | | ✔ | (20) |

それぞれの限定詞の用例を，(12) 以降にあげます.

(12) a. There is built-in storage space in *all* bedrooms. ［可算名詞の肯定文］

   b. *All* people are not as smart as you make them out to be.

                                       ［可算名詞の否定文. 部分否定］

   c. She'd given up *all* hope of having a child. ［不可算名詞の肯定文］

   d. Have you spent *all* your money? ［不可算名詞の疑問文］

## ＜もっと詳しく＞ ☞『**現代高等英文法**』p. 318
「all の文中での位置」

(13) a. *Every* student was given a prize. ［可算名詞の肯定文］

   b. *Each* factor is not mutually exclusive. ［可算名詞の否定文］

   c. You *each* are going home with a television.

   d. *Each* of us is / are responsible for building and effecting culture in our community.

(13c, d) が示すように，each は単数扱いが原則ですが，単数・複数両方が呼応することがあります.

(14) a. Did you get *many* responses to your advertisement?

                                    ［可算名詞の疑問文］

   b. Do you get *much* chance to travel in your job?

                                 ［不可算名詞の疑問文］

   c. Some of those houses have bathrooms but *many* do not.

   d. There are plenty of bars, *many* **of** them serving excellent food.

   e. I don't pretend to know *much* about art.

   f. *Much* **of** the evidence was gathered in 1991.

(14a, b) にあるように，many は可算名詞の数が多い，much は不可算名詞の量が多い，の意味で使用されます.(14c, e) の many, much は，限定詞の限定する名詞が省略されて，many, much が代名詞の役割を果たしています.(14d,

f) は, of … を伴う部分詞の働きをしています.

(15) a.　I have *some* money left, but not much.　　　[不可算名詞の肯定文]

　　 b.　The plants are inspected for insects and if I find *any*, they are
　　　　 squashed.　　　　　　　　　　　　　　　　　　　[代名詞用法]

　　 c.　She says she's feeling *some* better.　　　　　　　[副詞用法]

　　 d.　*Any* food would be better than nothing at all.　[不可算名詞の肯定文]

　　 e.　I had *some* difficulty in learning to swim.　　[不可算名詞の肯定文]

　　 f.　You don't have *any* difficulty driving?　　　[不可算名詞の疑問文]

　　 g.　It was *some* party.　　　　　　　　　　　　　[可算名詞の肯定文]

　　 h.　Would you give *some* investment advice?　　[不可算名詞の疑問文]

　(15a, b) は数量を意味する some, any で, 不可算名詞・可算名詞両方に使用
できます. また, (15b) の any は, any の後にくる名詞（ここでは insects）が
省略された代名詞として使用されています（some も代名詞として使用されま
す）. (15c) の some は, 副詞 better を修飾する副詞です. このような some は
形容詞も修飾し, any も副詞・形容詞を修飾する副詞用法を持ちます. (15d) の
any は,「どれをとっても」の意味です. (15e, f) の some, any は「少しの程度」
を言う用法です. (15g) の some は,「少しの程度」から発展した「かなり, 相
当の」の意味を表す婉曲語として使用されています. (15h) は,「少しは」の意
味で使用されている some です. any も同じ意味で使用されることがあります
(Did you publish *any* poetry back in 1996? 但し, この疑問文では話し手は,
出版したことを知らないという前提があります. some が使用された場合は, 出
版したことを知っている前提で, 確認をする質問です).

(16) a.　Outside there are only *a few* streetlights.

　　 b.　There are *few* earthquakes at the moment.

　　 c.　There were hundreds of protestors, not *a few of* whom were
　　　　 women.

(17) a.　Can I give you *a little* advice?

　　 b.　There was *little* chance of them winning.

　　c.　I could hear only *a little of* what they were saying.

　(16) は「a few + 可算名詞」(肯定),「few + 可算名詞」(否定) の例, (17) は
「a little + 不可算名詞」(肯定),「little + 不可算名詞」(否定) の例です. (16c)
と (17c) の *a few of* ～, *a little of* ～ の few, little は, 名詞用法です. また,
few, little の比較変化は, (18) に示す通りです.

　(18) a.　few — fewer — fewest
　　　 b.　little — less — least

　a few, few にはない用法として, a little, little には副詞用法があります. 前者
は自由に形容詞, 副詞を修飾しますが, 後者には制限があります. (19) を見て
ください.

　(19) a.　The whole situation makes me *a little* nervous.
　　　 b.　She was *a little* disappointed with the job.

(19a) は「少し心配だ」, (19b) は「少しがっかりした」の意味になりますが, a
little を little に置き換えて, little nervous, little disappointed にしても,「ほと
んど心配なかった」,「ほとんどがっかりしなかった」という意味にはなりません.
little は,「形容詞・副詞の比較形や different, sort of ... などを修飾し, 程度を
弱める用法に限られる」ことがわかっています. しかし, なぜ little にのみこの
ような制限があるのかは明らかになっていません.
　no は, (20) に示すように「no + 可算名詞 / 不可算名詞」,「no + 何らかの評価
を伴う名詞」,「no + 形容詞 / 副詞の比較級」の形式で使用されます.

　(20) a.　*No* trains will be affected by this incident.
　　　 b.　There's *no* milk, there's *no* soap, there's *no* sugar, there's *no* toilet
　　　　　paper.
　　　 c.　He's *no* fool.
　　　 d.　We played *no* better or worse than usual.

# ◉練習問題◉

1　形容詞型 It is Adj. that, NP be Adj. that, It is Adj. to do, NP is
　　Adj. to do, NP is Adj. PrepP を活用して自由に英作しなさい.

It is Adj. that: _____

NP be Adj. that: _____

It is Adj. to do: _____

NP is Adj. to do: _____

NP is Adj. PrepP: _____


2　以下の英文で使用されている形容詞 (beautiful, honest) は, 一時性もしく
　　は永続性のどちらか述べなさい.

(1) a.　She is beautiful enough to turn men's heads.

　　b.　The garden was so beautiful that she began to like it more than any-
　　　　thing else.

_____

(2) a.　It's great that you are being honest with yourself.

　　b.　I like people who are honest and principled and who care about oth-
　　　　ers.

_____


3　Oral translation: (　　) 内の語句を使用して英語にしなさい.

3.1　そんな事は, 3歳の子供にはわからない.　(That ...)

_____

3.2　きっと次の台風は, 紀伊半島に上陸するでしょう.　(hit / the Kii Peninsula)

_____

3.3　彼が経済学原論の単位を落としたとは, 驚きだ.　(the Principles of Eco-
　　nomics course)

_____

3.4　父は気難しいので困っている．（be in trouble）

---

3.5　10 キロを泳ぐなんて私には不可能です．

---

3.6　地震が起こった時に，君がすぐにガスを止めたのは賢明だった．（turn off the gas）

---

3.7　きれいな花を見ると，心が安らぎます．（comforting）

---

3.8　しばらくテニスをしていない．やりたくってうずうずしている．

---

# 第4章　副詞と副詞的語句

（『現代高等英文法』pp. 350 ～ 361 に該当）

## 1　副詞とは

　副詞は，文全体，動詞（句），副詞（句），形容詞（句），名詞句を修飾します．また，文の一部となって意味や機能を補う場合もあります．その中には，動詞句，副詞句，形容詞句，名詞句からなるものもあり，これを副詞的語句と呼びます．本章でいう副詞とは，副詞と副詞的語句を併せたものです．本章は，機能と意味の視点から副詞の実態を説明します．

## 2　副詞の種類 —— 機能と統語的特徴

　副詞は，Table 3.4.1 の4種類に分けられます．

Table 3.4.1　4 種類の副詞とそれらの機能と統語的特徴

| 種類 | 機能と統語的特徴 | 用例 |
|---|---|---|
| 付加詞<br>(adjunct) | 第 I 文型 S V A の A, 第 III 文型 S V O A の A のように文の意味を完成するために必要な要素<br>句動詞 (get up, sit down) の up, down など<br>疑問副詞 when, where, how, why<br>接続詞 when, where, how, why が導く節全体 | (1) |
| 下接詞<br>(subjunct) | 文全体，動詞 (句)，副詞 (句)，形容詞 (句)，名詞句を修飾する<br>強意の very 等，否定語 not, at all, quite, much, pretty, too, completely, extremely などの数量・程度を表す，主節の行為を行う目的を述べる | (2) |
| 離接詞<br>(disjunct) | 文の内容についての話し手の考えを述べる<br>Yes, No, admittedly, assuredly, candidly, certainly, evidently, surely, truly, just between you and me, to be frank with you, from one's point of view, according to, to the best of my knowledge など | (3) |
| 接合詞<br>(conjunct) | 文と文，あるいは前言の内容と次の内容を繋ぐ，接続詞と協力して文の流れをスムーズにする<br>anyway, thus, therefore, instead, moreover, nevertheless など | (4) |

(1) a. She lived *in Chicago*.

　　b. *When* did you see him yesterday?

　　c. *When I was young*, I lived in New York.

(2) a. He *kindly* offered me a ride.

　　b. I'm *very* tired.

　　c. I am *not* interested in it *at all*.

　　d. You are *quite* right about that.

　　e. I had to take 24 units *to sit for the exam*.

(3) 　*Sadly*, the storm destroyed the entire tobacco crop.

(4) a. I no longer have the support of the committee. I have *therefore*

decided to resign.

b. This is one possible solution to the problem. *However*, there are others.


# 3　意味による副詞の分類

ここでは，前節で提示した4つの副詞を，意味の視点から分類します.


## 3.1　付加詞

付加詞は，「時」「時間」「場所」「距離」を意味します. それぞれの例を (5)，(6)，(7)，(9) に示します. (9) の「距離」については，用例で提示します.

(5)　「時」: today, tonight, tomorrow, yesterday, the second morning, last year, next Monday, next month, tomorrow night, on Monday, in the morning, on Monday morning, on my birthday, at five o'clock, at night, by day, by night, a couple of years ago など

(6)　「時間」: (for) a moment, (for) a second, for seven years, during my stay in London, over the weekend, in a week, within a week など

時間を意味する付加詞は，「for／during／over＋名詞（句）」で使用される傾向にあります.

(7)　「場所」: here, there, in the garden, in Osaka, in the Kinki district, at Osaka station, in the east, toward north, abroad, downtown, outside, home, right, left など

(7) にあげたもののうち，abroad, downtown, outside, home, right, left は (8) のように用いられます.

(8) a. go *abroad* / *downtown* / *outside*

    b. stay *home*（アメリカ用法．イギリス用法は stay at home となり，この home は名詞）

    c. go / come *home*

    d. keep *right* / *left*（アメリカ用法．イギリス用法は keep to the right / left と right / left を名詞にする）

(9) a. Chicago was *about sixteen miles away from there*.

    b. I ran out of gas about *half way here*, but fortunately I could find a gas station near there.

    c. They walked *the length of the hall* and bowed to the old man.

## 3.2 下接詞

下接詞の代表的なものとして，very, much, a lot, lots があります．これら以外に，否定辞 not, never があります．本節は，まず代表的な very, much, a lot, lots と否定辞 not, never を説明します．その後，「頻度」「程度」「制限」を意味する下接詞を紹介します．とりわけ「程度」を意味する副詞はたくさんあります．

### 3.2.1 very, much, a lot, lots

very は，I'm *very* tired. のように形容詞・副詞の意味を強めます．次に，much は Table 3.4.2 のように 4 つの機能があります．

Table 3.4.2 much の 4 つの機能

| | 機能 | 用例 |
|---|---|---|
| ① | -ed 形の動詞・形容詞を修飾し，「幅広く」の意味で使用される | (10) |
| ② | 動詞句の意味を強める<br>否定文で使用され very を伴うことが多い．肯定文では a lot, lots が使用される． | (11) |
| ③ | 比較級の程度を強める | (12) |
| ④ | 前置詞句，as, like が導く節の意味を強める | (13) |

(10)　His father was *much* respected in that pretty town.

(11) a.　I didn't enjoy the film very *much*.

　　　b.　I enjoyed it *a lot*.

(12)　This book is *much* easier to read than that.

(13) a.　She was, *much* to my surprise, bigger than me both in terms of height and strength.

　　　b.　We use our language and culture *much* as we use the air to sustain our lives.

a lot, lots は話し言葉で使用される傾向にあり，Table 3.4.2 の①，②，③の役割を果たします．

(14) a.　That phrase is used *a lot*.　（①の用法）

　　　b.　I'm feeling *a lot* better today.　（③の用法）

　very は much の①の機能を持ちますが，意味的には -ed 形の動詞・形容詞の意味を強めます．それに対して，much/a lot は「量的な多さ」や「幅広さ」を表します．(15) に示す 2 つの意味の違いを考えてみてください．

(15) a.　I'm very tired.

　　　b.　I'm tired a lot.

## ＜もっと詳しく＞　☞『現代高等英文法』p. 356
「very much, pretty much」

### 3.2.2　否定辞 not, never
　否定辞は，否定の範囲があります．(16) の例を見てください．

(16) a.　I did*n't* <u>buy it</u> because it was too expensive.

　　　b.　I did*n't* appoint him <u>just because he was my son</u>.

(16a) の not は下線部 buy it を否定していますが，(16b) の not は下線部の理由を表す副詞節 just because 節を否定しています．このように否定の範囲が異

なります．同じような例を (17) と (18) にあげますので，意味の違いを考えて
ください．

(17) a.　I slept until nine.

b.　I didn't sleep until nine.

(18) a.　I stayed there until nine.

b.　I didn't stay there until nine.

(17b) の sleep は，寝ている状態の始まりの時が否定され，(18b) の stay は滞
在の終わりの時が否定されています．

もう一つの否定辞 never は，*Never* have I seen him since then. のように，文
頭に来た場合には倒置を起こします．また最近の英語の傾向として，否定辞
never の位置が変化しています．(19) の例を見てください．

(19)　I *never* could have made it without you.

（本来は I could never have made ....）


### 3.2.3　頻度

頻度を意味する副詞は，次のようなものがあります．各副詞の頻度順も併せて
提示します．

低い ◀━━━━━━━━━━━━━━━━━━━━━━━▶ 高い

never  hardly ever  seldom  scarcely  occasionally  frequently  often  usually  always
　　　 rarely　　　　　　　　　　　　　 sometimes


### 3.2.4　程度

程度を意味する副詞は，数多く存在します．下記に示すように 6 種類に分け
られます．

① 少ないことを意味する副詞：「a +「少し」の意味の名詞」のパタン

**a bit** + like, longer, better, less, different, later, further, odd, late など

**a crack** + open

**a fraction** + closer, faster, brighter, taller, harder, calmer, quieter など

**a pinch** + stronger など

**a shade** + darker, lighter, more, less, paler, closer, larger, redder, bluer, whiter など

**a little** + less, better, different, longer, late, nervous, later, closer, easier, harder など

② **kind of** + 形容詞 + 名詞　　　例：*a kind of* magic number

　(a) **kind of** + 形容詞 / 副詞 / 動詞

　　　例：The room was *kind of* dark. / She was *a kind of* very snobbish. /
　　　　　I actually *kind of* feel bad for him.

③ that が形容詞を修飾する場合

　　　例：I'm not *that* big on talking.

④ 「ずっと，はるかに」を意味する比較級を修飾する much, far

　　　例：I'm *much* [*far*] more interested in a trip to Australia than to Europe.

⑤ 「全く」を意味し，形容詞，副詞，前置詞句，接続詞が導く節を修飾する all

　　　例：You shouldn't be sitting there *all* **alone**.

　　　　　I'm *all* **in favour of** giving children more freedom.

⑥ 「全く」を意味し，名詞句，形容詞，副詞（形容詞・副詞とも段階性を持たない）を修飾する quite

　　　例：It was *quite* **a surprise** for me.

　　　　　It was a *quite* **huge** public school about 1000 students in it.

### 3.2.5　制限の only

この only は，「ただ…だけ」の意味で，修飾する語句の直前に使用されます。

(20) a.　He died *only* a week ago.

　　 b.　I *only* want orange juice.

　　 c.　I want *only* orange juice.

### 3.2.6　様態副詞

(21) のイタリックの様態副詞は，動詞を修飾しています.

(21) a.　I think he is wrong, but it is all right for you to think *differently*.

　　 b.　The car ran *headlong* into the fence.

上記の副詞以外に，手段の by, by means of, 理由の as, because, since, now that, for 節（PART III 第 7 章を参照してください），目的を意味する程度の副詞が存在します.


## 3.3　離接詞

離接詞は，文全体に対して，話し手の気持ちを表現する副詞で，文頭もしくは文中に用いられます.（22）を参照してください.

(22) a.　*Luckily*, the museum was not damaged by the earthquake.

　　 b.　The second incident *allegedly* occurred in the spring of 1992.

　　 c.　Winston Churchill *famously* said, "Give us the tools, and we will finish the job."

(22c) の famously は離接詞としての機能は持ちませんが，famously said とすることでこのフレーズ全体が離接詞の役割を果たします.

離接詞として，話し手の確信の度合いを表す副詞があります. 下記に，度合いの高低とともに表示します.

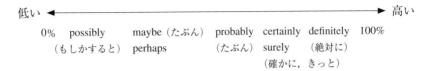

| 低い | | | | 高い |
|---|---|---|---|---|
| 0%　possibly | maybe（たぶん） | probably | certainly definitely | 100% |
| 　（もしかすると）| perhaps | （たぶん）| surely　　（絶対に）| |
| | | | （確かに，きっと）| |


## 3.4　接合詞

接合詞は，字の如く，文と文，あるいは前言の内容と次の内容を繋ぎ，文の流

れをスムーズにします．接続詞とともに使われることもあります．(23) の例を
見てください．

(23) a.　He was a carpenter, then *for some reason or other*, he decided to
become a cobbler.

b.　Phone home, *otherwise* your parents will start to worry.

c.　It seemed an impossible task at times, but we carried on, *regardless*.

(23b) は，「命令文＋or ～」と同じ意味で使用されます．(23c) は，carry on(,)
regardless の形で用いられることが多く，「それでもなお続ける」という意味です．

# ◉練習問題◉

1　I'm very tired. と I'm tired a lot. の意味の違いを説明しなさい．

I'm very tired. : ＿＿＿＿＿＿＿＿＿＿＿＿＿＿＿＿＿＿＿＿＿＿＿＿

I'm tired a lot. : ＿＿＿＿＿＿＿＿＿＿＿＿＿＿＿＿＿＿＿＿＿＿＿＿＿

2　以下の英文の違いを説明しなさい．

(1) a.　I slept until nine.

b.　I didn't sleep until nine.

＿＿＿＿＿＿＿＿＿＿＿＿＿＿＿＿＿＿＿＿＿＿＿＿＿＿＿＿＿＿＿

＿＿＿＿＿＿＿＿＿＿＿＿＿＿＿＿＿＿＿＿＿＿＿＿＿＿＿＿＿＿＿

(2) a.　I stayed there until nine.

b.　I didn't stay there until nine.

＿＿＿＿＿＿＿＿＿＿＿＿＿＿＿＿＿＿＿＿＿＿＿＿＿＿＿＿＿＿＿

＿＿＿＿＿＿＿＿＿＿＿＿＿＿＿＿＿＿＿＿＿＿＿＿＿＿＿＿＿＿＿

**3　確信の度合いを表す副詞，頻度副詞を利用して，自身の行動を英作しなさい.**
確信の度合いを表す副詞を使用した英文：

_____

頻度副詞を使用した英文：

_____


**4　Oral translation:（　　）内の語句を使用して英語にしなさい.**
4.1　オレンジジュースだけでいいです.

_____

4.2　ヘンリーがちょっと前に携帯電話でメールを送ってきた.（text-message）

_____

4.3　新幹線で新大阪駅に着くから，駅に迎えに来てください.

_____

4.4　ドアがちょっと開いて，猫が入ってきた.

_____

4.5　先日は，病気で休んで会議に出られずすいませんでした.

_____

4.6　私は，日曜日の午前中はテニスをすることにしています.

_____

4.7　予約なしに山田先生の研究室に行ったが，幸い先生はいた.

_____

4.8　アメリカにいる友達から，昨日ようやく本が届いた.（after waiting a long time）

_____

4.9　私の考え方は，あなたとは全く違います.

_____

4.10　私は決して飲酒運転はしません.

_____

# 第5章 比較

（『現代高等英文法』pp. 362 〜 372 に該当）

本章は，形容詞と副詞の応用である比較変化について説明します．

## 1 比較変化の作り方

比較変化には規則変化と不規則変化があり，比較級（comparative）と最上級（superlative）となります．

### 1.1 規則変化

規則変化は，Table 3.5.1 に示す作り方をします．基本的な作り方として，発音が短い単語はその単語に -er をつけて比較級を作成し，-est をつけて最上級を作ります．長い単語は，その単語に more をつけて比較級を作成し，most をつけて最上級とします．

Table 3.5.1　規則変化の作り方

| | 原級 | 比較級 | 最上級 | 作り方の説明 |
|---|---|---|---|---|
| 1音節 | small | smaller | smallest | 基本的な変化 |
| | large | larger | largest | 語尾が e で終わる場合 |
| | big | bigger | biggest | 子音を重ねる |
| 2音節 | angry | angrier | angriest | -y の y を i にかえて er, est をつける |
| | lazy | lazier | laziest | |
| | slowly | more slowly | most slowly | 形容詞に -ly を加えた副詞の変化 |
| 3音節以上 | interesting | more interesting | most interesting | 基本的な変化 |
| | unhappy | unhappier | unhappiest | 3 音節以上の語でも，un- で始まる形容詞は規則変化をする |
| | unhealthy | unhealthier | unhealthiest | |

## 1.2　不規則変化

不規則変化は，Table 3.5.2 にあるようにわずかです．

Table 3.5.2　不規則変化

| 原級 | 比較級 | 最上級 |
|---|---|---|
| good / well | better | best |
| bad / ill / badly | worse | worst |
| many / much | more | most |
| little（少し）* | less | least |
| far | farther / further | farthest / furthest |
| old | older / elder | oldest / eldest |

*「小さい」を意味する little は，規則変化（little—littler—littlest）をします．

## 2　比較の種類

比較は，意味から分類すると (1) の同等比較 (equal comparison)，(2) の優
勢比較 (superior comparison)，(3) に示す劣勢比較 (inferior comparison)，(4)
にある同定比較 (identity comparison) があります.

(1)　She is *as tall as* me.　(me の代わりの I/I am は堅い言い方)

(2)　She is *taller* than me.　(me の代わりの I/I am は堅い言い方)

(3)　Women were reportedly *less happy* than they used to be.

(4)　He's more friendly *than* helpful.

(1) から (3) の比較は，同じ尺度で 2 つのものを比較しています. (4) は，He
is friendly. という命題と He is helpful. という命題を比較し，helpful よりも
friendly のほうが彼を描写するには適切であるという同定 (identity) の仕方を比
較しています.

### ＜もっと詳しく＞　☞『現代高等英文法』p. 365
「than, as の後の代名詞の格」

### 2.1　同等比較

同等比較 (equal comparison) の表現として，(5a) の as … as (肯定文)，(5b)
の not as/so … as (否定文)，(5c) の not/never such … as/like (… には名詞
(句) が来て，as の後は節，like の後に名詞句が原則としてくる) があります.

(5) a.　J.J. is *as* tall *as* his brother.

　　 b.　Our teacher is *not as/so* old *as* everyone thinks him to be.

　　 c.　I have *never* seen *such* a beautiful girl *as* you are/*like* you.

(5) 以外に，「as much + 名詞 (句) + as」で名詞の度合いの同等比較ができま
す. (6) を見てください.

　(6)　He's *as much* a thief *as* I am.

(6) は,「彼も私と同じ程度に泥棒だ」という意味になりますが,両者が本当に泥棒かどうかはわかりません. ここでは,彼と私の度合いが同じであることを表現しています.

　倍数表現は,「倍数 + as … as」で表現します (例 : The price of gasoline in Europe is about **three times** *as* high *as* in the United States.).

　次に説明する as … as any (other) … の同等比較表現は,「(他の) どれと比べても同じ程度」の意味を表します. 最上級の意味ではありませんので注意をしてください.

　(7)　a.　I believe our boys are *as* good *as any* in the world.

　　　　b.　I strongly feel that sex education is just *as* important *as any other* type of education.

(8) に示す as … as anything は,「とても」という意味を表し,強意副詞の下接詞 (PART III 第 4 章) です.

　(8)　a.　He's *as* fat *as anything*.

　　　　b.　I felt *as* pleased *as anything*.

　上記の同等比較の表現をまとめると,(9) のようになります.

　(9)　a.　as … as

　　　　b.　not as / so … as

　　　　c.　not / never such … as / like

　　　　d.　as much … as

　　　　e.　倍数 + as … as

　　　　f.　as … as any (other) …

　　　　g.　as … as anything

## 2.2　優勢比較

優勢比較 (superior comparison) とは, The book is *more interesting* than any other book I have ever read. のような他のものとの差を表します. 優勢比較は, ①比較級を使用して表現する場合と, ②最上級を使用して表現する場合に分けられます.

### 2.2.1　比較級の使用

2つのものを of を使用して比較する場合, John is **the** *taller* **of the two.** のように選択肢を of で表し, 比較級でも the を用います.

#### 2.2.1.1　「the＋比較級 …, the＋比較級〜.」

「the＋比較級 …, the＋比較級〜.」は,「…であればあるほど〜」を意味します. (10) を参照してください.

　(10)　*The greater* the pressure (is), *the higher* the temperature (becomes).

#### 2.2.1.2　否定形

She is more hard-working than me. を否定にする場合, (11) の文法形式があります.

　(11)　a.　She is **not** *more hard-working* than me.

　　　　b.　She is **no** *more hard-working* than me.

　　　　c.　She is **not any** *more hard-working* than me.

(11a) は, 普通の優勢比較の否定文です. (11b) は, no が比較級の more を否定して「以上であることはない. 同等かそれ以下」の意味になります. (11c) は (11b) と同じ意味で, no を not any に置き換えたものです.

### 2.2.2　最上級の使用

時に2つの物を比較する場合にも最上級が用いられます (例：He is **the**

*youngest* (of the two brothers).). ただし，この the は使用されないこともあります．上述した The book is *more interesting* than any other book I have ever read. を最上級を使用して表現すると，The book is *the most interesting* of all the books I have ever read. となります．

### 2.2.3　優勢比較を修飾する副詞と強める語

下接詞に分類される副詞 a bit, a deal は，優勢比較を修飾します．また，easily the best/biggest などの決まった表現は，優勢比較を強めます．(12) にその例を示します．

(12) a.　She is **easily** *the most intelligent* person in the class.

b.　His second son was **easily** *the more ambitious and dangerous* of the two.

### 2.2.4　独立比較

独立比較 (absolute comparison) は，特定のものとの比較ではなく，度合いが高いことを，比較級もしくは最上級のどちらかを使用して表現します．(13) を参照してください．

(13) a.　Recently *more and more* foreigners want to learn both spoken and written Japanese.

b.　She is *a most efficient* publisher.

## 2.3　劣勢比較

劣勢比較 (inferior comparison) は，程度が劣っていることを表します．little —less—least, bad/ill—worse—worst が，これに該当します．これ以外の形容詞・副詞は，「less/least + 形容詞/副詞」で劣勢比較を表します．劣勢比較の文法形式は，優勢比較と変わりありません．(14) を見てください．

(14) a.　Her younger sister is *no less brilliant* than she is.

   b.  Of the two dogs, the child chose *the less expensive.*

   c.  *The more* we looked at the abstract painting, *the less* we liked it.

   d.  He became *less and less interested* in study.


## 2.4　同定比較

　同定比較（identity comparison）とは，1つのものについて X か Y のどちら
の表現が適切かを認定するものです．(15) の例のように，適切な方（＝X）を比
較級で表現します．

  (15)  a.  The river is ***wider*** than it is **deep**.

        b.  This is ***more sweet*** than it is **sad**.

        c.  She's ***more sick*** than **lazy**.

　(15) 以外の表現方法として，①名詞句の比較，②名詞の抽象化による比較，
③フレーズによる比較の 3 パターンがあります．①を (16)，②を (17)，③を
(18)，(19) に示します．

  (16)  a.  Music is *more* a way of life *than* an interest.

        b.  This is *more* a war movie *than* a western.

  (17)    He regards himself as *more* teacher *than* scholar.

  (18)  a.  What she did was *more of* a mistake *than* a crime.

        b.  It was *more of* a holiday *than* a training exercise.

  (19)  a.  Carbon dioxide is *no more* a pollutant *than* nitrogen is.

        b.  Death is *no less* a miracle *than* a birth is.

(19a) は X no more A than B のフレーズであり，「B と同様 A でない」と A,
B の両方を否定しています．教室で教えられる英語の代表的な英文の 1 つであ
る A whale is no more a fish than a horse is は，(19a) と同類です．(19b) の
X no less A than B は「B と同様 A である」と A, B の両方を肯定しているフ
レーズです．

# ◉練習問題◉

1　以下の同等比較のフレーズを利用して，自由に英作しなさい.

a. as … as: _____

b. not as / so … as: _____

c. not / never such … as / like: _____

d. as much … as: _____

e. 倍数 + as … as: _____

f. as … as any（other）… : _____

g. as … as anything: _____


2　The book is more interesting than any other book I have ever read. を，（1）such を使用した同等比較の英文，（2）最上級を使用した英文に書き換えなさい.

（1）_____

（2）_____


3.　フレーズ as good as it gets が使用された This is as good as it gets. の意味を述べなさい.

_____

_____

_____


4　Oral translation:（　　）内の語句を使用して英語にしなさい.

4.1　春と秋ではどちらが好きですか？

4.2　現在，100 メートル走ではウサイン・ボルトが世界で一番早い.（Usain Bolt, so far）

_____

4.3 今日食べた中華料理は，この前の中華街で食べたのと同じくらい美味しかった．

    ————————————————————————————————

4.4 ネス湖を見たとき，こんな美しい湖は見たことがないと思った．(Loch Ness)

    ————————————————————————————————

4.5 アメリカの前大統領は，誰だか知っていますか？

    ————————————————————————————————

4.6 オレゴン州のポートランドは，アメリカで一番美しい街の1つと言われている．(Portland)

    ————————————————————————————————

4.7 このパソコンは，新品同様です．

    ————————————————————————————————

4.8 このケーキは，見た目の半分も美味しくありません．

    ————————————————————————————————

4.9 時間がないから，これ以上はもう待てません．

    ————————————————————————————————

4.10 彼はもっと分別があると誤解をしていました．(know better)

    ————————————————————————————————

# 第6章　関係詞と疑問詞

（『現代高等英文法』pp. 328 〜 349 に該当）

　本章は，how も含めて *wh*-word 語（who, whose, whom, which, what, when, where, why, how）と呼ばれる関係詞（relative）と疑問詞（interrogative）について，説明します．

## 1　関係詞の概説

　関係詞は，①節と節を結びつける接続詞としての働き，②代名詞，副詞，形容詞の働き，の2つを持っています．関係詞は，関係代名詞，関係副詞，関係形容詞の総称です．この関係詞には，形容詞と同じように限定用法と叙述用法があります．関係詞が限定したり叙述したりする名詞句を先行詞（antecedent）と呼びます．(1) を見てください．

(1) a.　She has a brother *who* is now in London.　　[関係代名詞，限定用法]

　　 b.　She has a brother, *who* is now in London.　　[関係代名詞，叙述用法]

(2) a.　This is the house *where* Washington was born. [関係副詞，限定用法]

　　 b.　We then moved to Paris, *where* we lived for six years.

　　　　　　　　　　　　　　　　　　　　　　　　　　　　　[関係副詞，叙述用法]

(3) a.　She asked friends *whose* opinion she respected.

　　　　　　　　　　　　　　　　　　　　　　　　　　　[関係形容詞，限定用法]

　　 b.　The man, *whose* identity was not released, was attacked at 10 p.m. last night.　　　　　　　　　　　　　　　　　　　[関係形容詞，叙述用法]

上述しましたが，関係詞は2つの節から成り立っています．(1a), (2a), (3b)

の英文の成り立ちは，下記の通りです．

(1a) She has a brother + He is now in London.

a brother と he は同じなので，代名詞 he の代わりの関係代名詞 who
に変換し，節の先頭に移動

→ She has a brother, who is now in London.
　　　　先行詞　　関係代名詞

(2a) This is the house. + Washington was born there.

the house と there は同じ物をさすので，副詞 there の代わりの関係副
詞 where に変換し，節の先頭に移動

→ This is the house, where Washington was born.
　　　　先行詞　　関係副詞

(3a) She asked friends. + She respected their opinion.

friends と their は同じ物をさすので，形容詞 their の代わりの関係形
容詞 whose に変換し，節の先頭に移動

→ She asked friends whose opinion she respected.
　　　　先行詞　関係形容詞

　次に，関係代名詞，関係副詞，関係形容詞の限定用法と叙述用法について説明
します．(1a) は，She has several brothers, and one of them is now in London.
を含意しているので，兄弟が複数人いて，そのうちの 1 人がロンドンにいるこ
とがわかります．それに対して (1b) は，She has a brother, and he is now in
London. を含意しているため，兄弟が 1 人で，その 1 人がロンドンにいること
がわかります．(2b) の Paris や (3b) の the man のように先行詞が固有名詞や
特定のものをさす名詞は，限定用法の関係詞節に修飾されることはありません．

## ＜もっと詳しく＞　☞『現代高等英文法』p. 331
「叙述用法の関係詞の前のカンマは必須か？」

## 1.1　関係代名詞

関係代名詞（relative pronoun）には，who, whom, which, that, what, whatever, whichever があります．また，関係詞を使用せずに，2 つの節を結合する場合もあります．このような場合，「ゼロ関係詞」が接合していると考えます．本書は，ゼロ関係詞は φ を使用して表します．(4) を見てください．

(4) a.　I'm sure there'd be a lot more people *who*'d be better qualified than myself.

　　b.　Was she another of the ex-soldiers *whom* Dennison had recruited from the army?

　　c.　This is the personal computer *which* I bought at the electric appliances store.

　　d.　The sun *that* ripens the crops is a big benefit to us.

　　e.　That's the job φ I could never do.

(4) では，関係代名詞はイタリック体で表記していますが，それぞれの先行詞はどれか考えてみてください．

### 1.1.1　who, whom, that, φ

(1) のように先行詞が人で主格の場合は who, 目的格の場合は whom となります．しかし，この whom の代わりに，ゼロ関係詞になることがあります．ただし，many of whom のように前置詞の目的語になる場合は，whom が必要です（例：I have a lot of friends in America, *many of whom* are university students.）．

会話では目的格の whom の使用は堅苦しく，who を使うか whom を使うか迷うということがあるので，that を使用する傾向があります．この that の影響で，馴染みの表現である those who ～（～する人々）が，those that になることがあります．これ以外に，ゼロ関係詞の場合もあります．(5) を参照してください．

(5) a.　There might be people *that* we don't know of.

　　 b.　You're one person　φ I can talk to.

次に関係代名詞 that の特徴について説明します．that には (6) に示す特徴が
あります．

(6) a.　that は先行詞が人でも物でも，主格でも目的格でも使用される．

　　　　例：The guy *who/that* shouted must have been on about the sev-
　　　　enth floor.

　　　　This is the problem *which/that* we're having at the moment.

　　 b.　that には叙述用法はない．

　　　　例：We cannot decide whether tomatoes, *which/* × *that* we are all
　　　　fond of, are a fruit or a vegetable.

　　 c.　that は前置詞の直後には使用されない．

　　　　例：Economics, about *which/* × *that* so many books have been
　　　　written, is not really a dull subject.

　　 d.　先行詞が人と物の場合，関係代名詞は that が選択される．

　　　　例：There are blogs and books and people *that* always want to
　　　　advise you on how to be successful in law school.

　　 e.　先行詞に the only, 序数, the very, the last などの修飾語がある場
　　　　合，不定代名詞（any-, every-, no-）の複合語の場合と all の場合は，
　　　　who, which ではなく that が選択される．

　　　　例：I did the best job *that* I could.

関係代名詞は who, whom, that, φ が基本ですが，人を表す名詞を先行詞とす
る場合に which が使われることがあります．その場合，① [人を表す名詞＋
which] の形で叙述用法，② [人の団体を表す名詞＋which]，の 2 つの場合があ
ります．①の場合，人を表す名詞が人そのものでなく，人の性質や属性を表して
います．(7) の例を見てください．

(7) a.　They accused him of being a traitor, *which* he undoubtedly was.

　　 b.　Ignoring immigrants excludes a social group *which* already plays an important role in social and economic development.

(7b) の which は，団体を 1 つの集団としてみているため使用されています．構成員を念頭に置く場合は，who になります．

　which は人を先行詞とする以外に，他の関係詞にはない用法があります．それは，前の主節全体を先行詞とする用法です．(8) の例を見てください．(8) の which は，The student showed no interest in it という節を先行詞としています．

　(8)　The student showed no interest in it, *which* deeply disappointed me.

## ＜もっと詳しく＞　☞『**現代高等英文法**』p. 333f.
「誤用とされる whom, who」

### 1.1.2　自由関係代名詞
　先行詞を含んでいる関係代名詞を自由関係代名詞（free relative pronoun）と言います．what, whatever, who, whoever, whichever がそれに該当します．what, whatever は物，who, whoever は人，whichever は選択範囲が決まった中での物の選択の場合に使用されます．(9) を見てください．

　(9)　a.　Is this exactly *what* he said?
　　　b.　You can choose *whatever* you like.
　　　c.　She is not *who* she was ten years ago.
　　　d.　You can invite *whoever* you want.
　　　e.　Choose *whichever* you want.

#### 1.1.2.1　what, whatever の特徴
　自由関係代名詞 what は，(10) の特徴があります．

　(10)　a.　[that（先行詞）＋which（関係代名詞）] に置き換え可能．ただし，that which は堅苦しい言い方．
　　　　b.　「人の性質，属性，職業」を言う場合にも使用される．
　　　　　（例：*What* she became in later life distressed her friends.）

c.　what が導く関係詞節が，挿入句的な機能を果たすことがある.
　　（例：There are several gases that make up *what we call* "air" on planet earth.）

自由関係代名詞 whatever は，（11）の特徴があります.

(11) a.　[anything that] に書き換え可能.

　　 b.　whatever が導く関係節全体が副詞節の機能を果たす場合がある.
　　　（例：*Whatever you decide*, the principles are the same.）

**1.1.2.2**　who, whoever, whomever の特徴
自由関係代名詞 who は，（12）に示す特徴を持ちます.

(12) a.　the person who に言い換え可能.（例：You're not *who* I thought you were. → You're not *the person who* I thought you were.）

　　 b.　whoever, whomever と使い方が同じ any person who に言い換え可能. ただし，whomever は堅苦しい言い方. whichever も含めて，関係節の動詞は choose, like, please, want, wish に限られる.
　　　（例：She can marry *who/whoever/whomever* she pleases.）

**＜もっと詳しく＞**　☞ **『現代高等英文法』** p. 340f.
「as, than の接続詞用法」

**1.2　関係副詞**

関係副詞（relative adverb）は，Table 3.6.1 の種類と特徴があります.

Table 3.6.1 関係副詞一覧

| 関係副詞 | 意味 | 特徴 | 用例 |
|---|---|---|---|
| where | 場所 | 先行詞を取らない自由関係副詞になることがある | (13a) |
| | | ゼロ関係詞に置き換わることがある | (13b) |
| | | that が用いられることがある | (13c) |
| | | 叙述用法の際は and there の意味 | (13d) |
| when | 時 | 自由関係副詞になることがある | (14a) |
| | | ゼロ関係詞に置き換わることがある | (14b) |
| | | that が用いられることがある | (14c) |
| | | 叙述用法の際は and then の意味 | (14d) |
| how | 方法 | 先行詞なし | (15a) |
| | | how の代わりに the way が使用されることがある | (15b) |
| | | the way how（まれ） | |
| why | 理由 | the reason why / that | (16a) |
| | | 理由を言う節の接続詞が because になる | (16b) |
| whenever | …の時は いつでも | 先行詞を取らない自由関係副詞 | (17) |
| | | at any time when に置き換え可 | |
| wherever | …の場所は どこでも | 先行詞を取らない自由関係副詞 | (18) |
| | | at any place where に置き換え可 | |

(13) a. Macy's is *where* I buy my clothes.

　　 b. This is the place φ we'll raise our child.

　　 c. They know that this is the place *that* we were born and raised.

　　 d. He came from Brighton, *where* Lisa had once spent a holiday.

(14) a. The only time I see myself full-length is *when* I buy clothes.

　　 b. This is the time φ they make their money.

　　 c. Now is the time *that* we show the world that we are the toughest men on this planet.

d.  My favourite holiday was in 2009, *when* I went to Jamaica.

(15) a.  This is *how* he came to the conclusion that the murderer was the man.

b.  She also reveals that this is *the way* she herself grew up.

(16) a.  The reason *why* the injection needs repeating every year is that the virus changes.

b.  The reason *that* Obama "didn't say anything" during the debate is *because* he has a "strategy."

(17)  Never fail to drop in *whenever* (＝at any time when) you are around.

(18)  I'll go *wherever* (＝at any place where) you want me to.


## ＜もっと詳しく＞　☞『**現代高等英文法**』p. 342f.

「time, occasion; case, situation が先行詞の場合の関係副詞の選択」


### 1.3　関係形容詞

　関係形容詞 (relative adjective) には，what, which, whichever, whatever, whose があります．それぞれの用例を (19) にあげます．イタリック体の関係形容詞は，後続する名詞の限定詞の役割を果たしています．このような使われ方は，堅い表現法で，書き言葉で使用されます．

(19) a.  He has lost *what* little respect many people had for him.

b.  In 1960 he came to London, in *which* city he has lived ever since.

c.  *Whichever* book you borrow must be returned within a week.

d.  We're going to take *whatever* money we can and get out of here.

e.  The English Language, *whose* usefulness is known to all of us, is not necessarily easy to learn.

## 2　疑問詞の種類・役割

　疑問詞は，場所や時間，理由などを尋ねる際に使用されます．その疑問詞には，疑問代名詞，疑問形容詞，疑問副詞があります．疑問代名詞は，相手に質問したいことが人や物事の場合に使用されます．疑問形容詞は，what, which が名詞の前に来て，形容詞として働くものを指します．疑問副詞は，場所や時，理由を尋ねる副詞として使用される when, where, why, how のことです．これらをまとめると Table 3.6.2 のようになります．

Table 3.6.2　疑問詞一覧

| 疑問詞 | 主格 | 所有格 | 目的格 | 意味 | 対象 | 用例 |
|---|---|---|---|---|---|---|
| 疑問代名詞 | who | whose | whom | 誰の物 | 人 | (20) |
| | what | – | what | 何，どの | 物事 | |
| | which | – | which | どちら | 物事，人（which of 〜で） | |
| 疑問形容詞 | what | – | – | どんな | 物事 | (21) |
| | which | – | – | どちらの | 物事，人 | |
| | – | whose | – | 誰の | 人 | |
| 疑問副詞 | when | – | – | いつ | 時 | (22) |
| | where | – | – | どこ | 場所 | |
| | how | – | – | どのように | 程度・方法 | |
| | why | – | – | なぜ | 理由 | |

(20) a.　*Who*'s that guy with your wife?
　　 b.　*Whose* is this jacket?
　　 c.　To *whom* do you wish to talk?
　　 d.　*Which* do you like, tea or coffee?
　　 e.　*What* caused the accident?

  f. *Which/What* is the hottest city in the world?

(21) a. *What/Which* project do you choose?

  b. *Whose* fault is it that we are losing all this money?

  c. *Which* doctor do you want to see?

(22) a. *When* are you leaving?—I'm leaving *tomorrow.*

  b. *Where* do you live?—I live *in Tokyo.*

  c. *How* do you spell your name?—It's *A-N-T-H-O-N-Y.*

  d. *Why* are you angry?—*Because I don't like that man.*

 (20) のうち，(20a, b, c, d) は，それぞれ that guy, this jacket, you, you が主語となっているため，主語と操作詞の倒置が起きています．しかし，(20e, f) は疑問代名詞が主語となっているため，主語と操作詞の倒置は起きません．(20c) の whom は，who の目的格で動詞や前置詞の目的語として使用されていましたが，(20c) のように「前置詞＋whom」(e.g. one of whom, none of whom, some of whom) の形で使用される傾向にあり，非常に堅苦しい形式です．現在は，動詞や前置詞の目的語の場合でも前置詞を元の場所に置いたまま，who を文頭に使用します．

 (20) と (21) で使用されている which は，基本的には物について使用されます．しかし，(23) の場合は，which は人について使用されます．(23) を参照してください．

(23) a. 選択肢を問う … of が後続する場合

   e.g. *Which of your parents* do you feel closer to?

   （who of 〜 の形も使用されます）

  b. which を疑問形容詞として使用した which one/which boy, etc. の場合 = (21c)

  c. 前後の文脈で人の選択肢であることが明らかな場合

   e.g. *Who/Which* do you like best?—your father or your mother?

(23c) の場合，グループ内や集合写真の中から人を特定する場合は，which が使用されます (e.g. *Which* is your husband?—The one in jeans.)

┏━━ ！注意！ ━━━━━━━━━━━━━━━━━━━━━━━━━━┓

　相手に Who are you? と聞くのは，威圧的・侮辱的になるので特殊な事情がある場合以外は使用を避けたほうが賢明です．では，どのように聞けばよいかというと，May I have your name, please?（お名前をお伺いできますか？）です．また職業を問う場合は，"What do you do?", "What field are you in?" が使用できます．答え方は，I'm working on 〜./I'm in charge of 〜./I work in 〜. です．しかし，初対面の方には職業や年齢などの個人的な質問は極力避けることです．What are you? は，相手の非行を叱責する，相手を馬鹿にする，侮辱的に問い詰める際に使用される表現ですので，特別な事情がない限り使用は避けてください．

┗━━━━━━━━━━━━━━━━━━━━━━━━━━━━━━━━━┛

　疑問形容詞は，選択肢がわかっている場合には which，わかっていない場合は what が使用されます（= (21a)）．(21a) に示すように，which/what は名詞の前に来て形容詞の働きをし，what は「どの」，which は「どちらの」という意味で使用されます．what, which の意味を強調する場合は，whatever, whichever を使用します．

　(20b) の whose は疑問代名詞，(21b) の whose は疑問形容詞です．

　(22) の疑問副詞には，when（時），where（場所），how（方法），why（理由）の4つがあります．疑問副詞の場合，why 以外の疑問副詞の答えは部分的にわからないことを聞いているので，文の一部となり答え以外の部分は省略可能です．why の場合は，you are angry という話題の内容はすべて知っており，その理由を聞いているので because 以下全体が答えとなっています．why は whyever が存在しないというように，他の疑問副詞と異なる振る舞いをします．

## 2.1　why の特徴

　why は，①「動機を聞く」意味と ②「理由を聞く」意味があります．それぞれの特徴をまとめたものが，Table 3.6.3 です．

Table 3.6.3　why の特徴

| 意味 | 答え方 | その他の特徴 | 用例 |
|---|---|---|---|
| 動機を聞く why | to 不定詞,<br>so that 節,<br>because 節 | 操作詞と主語を省略し，原形<br>の動詞のみの文が可<br>動詞のない文が可<br>not で否定節の代用が可<br>why to do は不可 | (24),<br>(25),<br>(26) |
| 理由を聞く why | because 節 | why to do は不可 | (27) |

(24)　Why did you go to Tokyo yesterday?

　　a.　*To attend* the meeting.

　　b.　*So that* I wouldn't miss the meeting.

　　c.　*Because* I had to attend the meeting.

(25) a.　*Why* invite him? (← Why (do you) invite him?)

　　b.　*Why* no children?

　　c.　I don't read books.—*Why* not?

(26)　×I don't know *why to do it*.

(27)　Why is grass green?

　　*Because* it contains chlorophyll.

why 〜? と入れ替え可能と言われてきた how come S + V? は，実はそうではありません．how come S + V? は，了解済みの命題についての動機，意志，予定，許可を問う際，科学的根拠などの理由を問う際には使用されません．ですので，(27) の why 疑問文を how come に変えたもの (×How come grass is green?) は，使用されません．

how come S + V? は，命題についての予備知識をさらに発展させ，その動機等を驚き等をもって質問する疑問文です．つまり，(24) の Why did you go to Tokyo yesterday? は How come you went to Tokyo yesterday? に書き換え可能ですが，「どうして昨日東京に行くような羽目になったの？　そんなことは言ってなかったじゃないか」の意味になります．また，how come 疑問文は主語と動詞の語順転換をする必要がないため，操作詞は不要です．

# ◉練習問題◉

**1　以下の 2 つの文を，適切な関係詞を使用して 1 つの文にしなさい.**

a. She has a brother. / He is now in London.

_____

b. This is the house. / Washington was born there.

_____

c. She asked friends. / She respected their opinion.

_____

**2　以下の 2 つの例文を，[　　　] 内の語を用いて書き換えなさい.**

a. Is this exactly _what_ he said? [that which]

_____

b. To _whom_ do you wish to talk? [who]

_____

**3　関係副詞 where, when, how, why, whenever, wherever を使用して，自由に英作しなさい.**

where: _____

when: _____

how: _____

why: _____

whenever: _____

wherever: _____

**4　Oral translation:(　　) 内の語句を使用して英語にしなさい.**

4.1　この方が，今朝あなたを訪ねて来られた方です.

_____

4.2　アメリカ生まれの美奈子は，日本の生活様式になかなか慣れることができ
　　　ない．（get adjusted to ... ）

_____

4.3　私は高校生の時にある女の子を好きになったが，今では名前も忘れてし
　　　まった．

_____

4.4　この本を皆が欲しがっているが，今は絶版になっている．（be out of print）

_____

4.5　沖縄は，誰もが一度は夏に訪れたいと思う場所です．

_____

4.6　A: お誕生日プレゼントは何がいいですか？
　　　B: お花だったらなんでもいいです．（any flowers would be fine）

_____

_____

4.7　私は，こういう理由で会社を辞めました．（quit）

_____

4.8　彼は，いわゆる有名大学の卒業生だが，それが必ずしも彼の将来を約束す
　　　るわけではない．（what is known as）

_____

_____

4.9　かつて，日本人が住む家を見て「うさぎ小屋」と言った外国人がいた．（a
　　　rabbit hutch）

_____

4.10 日本語で「マンション」というのは英語で apartment / flat, あるいは condo-
　　　minium という．英語のマンションは，広大な敷地に建てられた豪壮な建
　　　物をいう．（a grand building, on a large estate）

_____

_____

# 第7章　接続詞と前置詞

（『現代高等英文法』pp. 373 ～ 380 に該当）

## 1　接続詞と前置詞

　接続詞と前置詞は，後ろに何が来るかで区別します．同じ語が，接続詞と前置詞で使用されることもあります．

Table 3.7.1　前置詞と接続詞の区別

| 接続詞：後ろに節<br>　　（S V）が来る | Several years *after* **they'd split up,** they met again by chance in Paris.<br>That happened *before* **he got married.** |
| --- | --- |
| 前置詞：後ろに句が<br>　　来る | *After* **winning the prize,** she became famous overnight.<br>That happened *before* **his marriage.** |

## ＜もっと詳しく＞　☞『現代高等英文法』p. 374

「前置詞，接続詞，副詞を区別しない考え方」

## 2　接続詞

　接続詞（conjunction）には，等位接続詞（coordinate conjunction）と従属接続詞（subordinate conjunction）があります．等位接続詞は and, but, or で，節や句を統語的に対等の関係で接続します．等位接続された文は重文（compound sentence）と言います．従属接続詞には多種多様なものがあり，意味もさまざま

です．従属接続詞に導かれる節を従属節と呼び，主節と従属節をもった文を複文 (complex sentence) と言います．

## 2.1  名詞節

that や wh- 語といった従属接続詞が導く節は，文の中で名詞の役割をします．

(1)  It is hard to accept **the fact** *that she's gone.*                    [同格節]

(2)  I **know** (*that*) *people's handwriting changes as they get older.*

[動詞の目的語]

(3)  **It's our view** *that women should get paid the same as men.*

[仮主語 it の指す真主語]

(4)  **It is** vitally **important** *that you should understand the danger.*

[仮主語 it の指す真主語]

(5)  We are **told** *when the two presidents meet at the White House.*

[間接疑問文：動詞の目的語]

(6)  I **know** *how difficult it is to read your thoughts.*

[間接感嘆文：動詞の目的語]

## 2.2  形容詞節

(7)  Imagine my **surprise** *when I woke up this morning and read his blog.*

(8)  **Language** *as we know it* is a unique human property.

(7) の when 節は，名詞句 my surprise を修飾する形容詞節です．imagine する時を表しているのではないので注意しましょう．(8) の as 節も「…する限りの」という意味で後ろから前の Language を修飾する形容詞節になっています．

## 2.3　副詞節

　副詞節として機能する従属節は，多様な接続詞が多様な意味で導きます．主に主節で述べられる出来事が起こった「時」や「期間」，「場所」を表したり，それが起こる「条件」を述べます．また，出来事や行為の「目的」や「理由」を述べます．「…しようとも」「…だけれども」という意味関係を表すのは「譲歩」です．「まるで…のようだ」といった「様態」や，「…するように」という「付帯」，「とても…ので〜である」といった「結果」を表すものもあります．

Table 3.7.2　副詞節を導く従属接続詞

| 時 | when, before, after, since, while, as, until, the moment, every time, each time, the last time, the next time など | (1) "Can I have a drink of water?"　"Not *until* you answer this question." <br> (2) She locked the house *when* she went out. <br> (3) She had not seen him *since* they were both sixteen. <br> (4) *The last time* we talked he said he needed another two days. <br> (5) I want to see him *the moment* he arrives. |
|---|---|---|
| 期間 | when, while など | (6) She was often nervous *when* (she was) facing the camera. |
| 条件 | if, unless, provided that など | (7) She won't believe him *unless* he can prove his theory. |
| 目的 | in order that, so that など | (8) The soldiers gave their lives *in order that* (= so that) we may live in a safer and more peaceful world. |
| 理由 | because, since, as, in case, just in case, for など | (9) He continued to eat the pancakes, *because* he was hungry. <br> (10) I had to cancel the appointment, *for* I had one of my Achilles' tendons ripped. <br> (11) Pretty *as* the dog was, it was loved by the family. <br> (12) Fool *that* I was, I believed him. |

| 譲歩 | as, although, though, even though, even if, while, whereas, whatever, wherever, however, except that, not that など | (13) *Though* the room was cool, I was bathed in sweat.<br>(14) *Whatever* the problem is, I'm sure I can help.<br>(15) Knowing him *as* I do, I can't believe he would do such a thing.<br>(16) Try *as* he might (＝However hard he tried), he couldn't open the door.<br>(17) Wilma could do better than Mr. Snyder, lovely man *though* he was. |
|---|---|---|
| 場所 | where, wherever など | (18) She carried it with her *wherever* she went. |
| 様態 | as, as though, as if, like, the way など | (19) I am going to talk to you *as though* you were quite grown up. |
| 付帯 | as など | (20) *As* I said before, many people are starving in Africa. |
| 結果 | so/such ... that など | (21) You are *so* smart *that* you can think of other ways to deal with this problem. |

**！注意！**

I think, I believe, you know, I'm afraid といった話し手の気持ちを表現する主節は，本来の位置から遊離して，従属節の中や末尾に使われることがあります．このようなものをコメント節と言います．

# 3  前置詞

前置詞（preposition）には，もともとから前置詞である基本前置詞（primary preposition）と別の品詞から派生して前置詞になった二次前置詞（secondary preposition) があります.

## 3.1 前置詞の種類

### Table 3.7.3 基本前置詞

| 前置詞 | after, at, by, for, from, in, of, one, to, off, out (of), over, since, through, till, under, up, with など |
|---|---|
| 前置詞＋別の要素から成り立つもの | about, above, across, against, along, alongside, amid, around, be-fore, behind, below, beneath, beside(s), between, beyond, inside (of), outside (of), into, onto, throughout, toward(s), underneath, until, upon, within, without など |

### Table 3.7.4 二次前置詞

| 現在分詞由来 | concerning, considering, during, excepting, following, owing to, regarding, respecting, notwithstanding など |
|---|---|
| 接続詞由来 | because of, but for など |
| 過去分詞由来 | except, past, granted など |
| 形容詞由来 | due to, like, minus, near (to), opposite to, round, less, unlike など |
| 群前置詞 | in back of, in front of, in spite of, in view of, by way of, by means of, on account of, on top of, in addition to, in return for, in/with regard to など |

ここでは 1 つひとつの前置詞を細かく取り上げることはしませんので, 辞書を活用してそれぞれの用法を調べてみましょう.

## 3.2 前置詞句の機能

前置詞句は文中で, 副詞の機能と形容詞の機能を果たします.

Table 3.7.5   前置詞句の機能

| 副詞用法 | | (1) I was *in London* when the earthquake hit Northern Japan.<br>(2) I was sightseeing *in London*.<br>(3) I am anxious *about how this will affect the weekend*. |
|---|---|---|
| 形容詞用法 | 叙述用法 | (4) It is *of great importance* to read as many books as you can while you are a student. |
| | 限定用法 | (5) My friends *in Hawaii* are all Samoans.<br>(6) My life *in New York* is a happy one. |

## ◉練習問題◉

1　各文のかっこに接続詞を入れなさい．日本語がある場合は日本語を参考にしなさい．

1.1　I was elected class president, (　　　　　) I told you on the phone.
（電話で言ったように）

1.2　She didn't notice him first (　　　　) she had not seen him since they were both sixteen.

1.3　I left a message at the door, just (　　　　) (　　　　) someone drops in while I'm away.
（留守中に誰か訪ねてくるといけないから）

1.4　We had been ready to get off our Shinkansen well (　　　　) it began to slow. （…する前に十分余裕をもって）

1.5　You don't have to (　　　　) you don't want to.
（やりたくなければ無理にしなくていいですよ）

**2 各文のかっこに，前置詞を入れなさい．日本語がある場合は日本語を参考にしなさい．**

2.1 The Delta variant was first identified (　　　) India (　　　) December 2020.

2.2 She took the smartphone (　　　) her everywhere she went.

2.3 I think I could be (　　　) help to you. (助けになる)

2.4 It was forty minutes (　　　) ten. (10時40分)

2.5 He glanced (　　　) the ring finger (　　　) my left hand.

2.6 I got in (　　　) the front door.

2.7 I left the room (　　　) a daze. (呆然として)

2.8 You'll meet many wonderful people (　　　) your lifetime. (生きている間に)

2.9 She has studied the subject (　　　) a long time and learned a lot (　　　) it.

2.10 Mary was (　　　) a chair (　　　) the window. (窓のそばの椅子に座っていた)


**3 Oral translation: (　) 内の語句を使用して英語にしなさい．**

3.1 私はうなずくだけで他には何も言いませんでした．

3.2 もし君がスケジュール通りにこだわるのであれば，僕は今やってることは全部やめないといけないかもしれない．
(stick to the schedule / drop everything)

3.3 30代の男性がオフィスから出てきたので，私が探していた人だと思いました．

3.4　父が一階に降りていってから1時間くらいすると,「夕食の準備ができた
　　　よ」と大声で言うのが聞こえました.

---

3.5　彼が野球をやっているのかはよく知らないけど, マラソンをやっているの
　　　はたしかだよ. (not sure whether / run marathons)

---

3.6　彼は, そこの家具はイケアのものだと言いました. (from Ikea)

---

3.7　エリックは僕のうわさを流し始めて, 学校中のみんなに僕がメアリーと付
　　　き合っていると言いふらした. (start a rumor about / be seeing)

---

3.8　「ここで何しているの?」
　　　「自転車でちょっとぶらついてたんだ」(be out / for a ride on my bike)

---

3.9　公園に着くまでに私は息が切れていた. (out of breath)

---

3.10　彼が誰のことを言っているのかはわかってたけど,「誰?」って聞いたんだ.
　　　(though / who he meant)

---

# ◎練習問題の答え◎

## PART I   文と文型

### 第1章   文，文型，文を構成する基本要素

**1   5文型を使用した英文を作成しなさい.**
自由解答

**2   p. 7にある (6) の英文 a ～ h の文型を書きなさい.**
(6) a. [I]　　b. [I]　　c. [III]　　d. [III]　　e. [III]　　f. [III]　　g. [V]　　h. [IV]

**3   Oral translation: 以下の日本文を，指定された文型と単語もしくはフレーズを活用して英語で言いなさい.**

3.1   Does this bus go downtown? / Do you go downtown? （運転手に聞く場合）

3.2   [I] There are twelve months in a year.

　　　[III] A year has twelve months.

3.3   This coffee smells good.

3.4   Professor Yamamoto is a specialist in English literature.

3.5   She mistook me for my twin sister.

3.6   [III] Do you think he is honest?

　　　[V] Do you think him honest?

3.7   How do you say 'kirin' in English? / What do you call 'kirin' in English? （what ～ ? のほうが普通に使用される.）

3.8   Have you ever found a four-leaf clover?

3.9   Could you tell me how tall that building is? / Could you tell me the height of that building?

3.10  Have you (already) paid her the debt yet?

3.11  His hair style always makes him look young.

3.12  He always leaves his hair unkempt.

3.13  [I] It will rain tomorrow morning.

　　　[II] It will be rainy tomorrow morning.

　　　[III] We will have rain tomorrow morning.

3.14  [I] It is said that colleges and universities in Japan are difficult to get into [enter] and easy to get out of [graduate from].

[III] They [People] say that colleges and universities in Japan are difficult to get into [enter] and easy to get out of [graduate from].

3.15 [I] It is said that a dragon lives in the lake at the top of the mountain.

[III] They [People] say that a dragon lives in the lake at the top of the mountain.

## 4 文の意味をよく考えて，（　　）内の動詞を［　　］内の指示に従って正しい態に変えなさい．

4.1 This picture is always admired.

4.2 His leg was hurt in an accident.

4.3 The answers must be written on this side of the paper only.

4.4 Has your question been answered?

4.5 Entering the crowded room, the woman could not see even one person whom she knew.

## 5 態を変えなさい．

5.1 Has the chair been fixed yet?

5.2 I was invited to their wedding reception.

5.3 He was seen to enter the store with his wife.

5.4 They ate up all the biscuits yesterday.

5.5 People say that several assembly members are involved in the bribery case.

## 第2章 修飾要素，独立要素，文の種類

## 1 単文，複文，重文，重複文を自由に英作しなさい．

自由解答

## 2 間接疑問文，エコー疑問文，let 命令文，間接感嘆文を自由に英作しなさい．

自由解答

## 3 Oral translation:（　　）内の指示に従って，訳しなさい．

3.1 （単文）Let's ask the man / woman how to get to the station.

（複文）Let's ask the man / woman how we can get to the station.

3.2 I'm good at reading English but poor at writing it. / I can read English well, but I can't write it well.

3.3 When you come across a word you don't know, look it up in a / the dictionary.

3.4 The weather report/forecast said that it would be sunny/a sunny day, but it has started raining.

3.5 Please text-message me tonight./Could you text-message me tonight?

3.6 We're/I'm going to have three days off starting tomorrow.

3.7 A: I would like to have a day off tomorrow.

B: You would like to have a what?

3.8 A: And you got off at what station?

B: San Diego.

3.9 Write with a ball-point pen not with a fiber-tip pen.

3.10 Do (exactly) as I say, or you'll fail the course/withdraw from the class.

## 4 （　　）の語句を使用して，日本語を英語に訳しなさい.

4.1 I already look forward to the summer vacation/holiday.

4.2 Tomorrow is the school foundation day, so we have a day off/so we have no class.

4.3 My economics class/lecture was canceled today and I'm going to study in the library.

4.4 We have had very few/only a few customers today, we weren't so busy at all.

4.5 We're expecting a lot of guests today. Don't come down from your room/downstairs./Stay in your room.

## PART II　述語動詞構成要素と準動詞

### 第1章　動詞と動詞型

## 1　動詞の ask は，どのような意味でどのような文型，動詞型で使用されるかを辞書で調べなさい.

| 尋ねる | S V<br>[第 I 文型] | Why didn't you ask?<br>I would have to tell anyone who asked that Tom was her father. |
| | S V O<br>[第 III 文型] | She asked a lot of difficult questions (of me).<br>They asked what happened.<br>They kept asking me about the deal. |
| | S V O O<br>[第 IV 文型] | She asked me a lot of awkward questions.<br>She asked me what had become of the money she had been paid for the picture.<br>He asked me if I liked reading books. |

| 頼む | S V O [第 III 文型] | He asked to be excused. |
| | | He asked that she (should) come with him. |
| | S V O C [第 V 文型] | She asked me to meet her at McDonald's near the station. |

| 求める, 請求する | S V [第 I 文型] | He went down on bended knee to ask for her hand in marriage. |
| | S V O [第 III 文型] | I'd like to ask a favor of you. |
| | | I was surprised when he asked me for 10,000 yen. |
| | S V O O [第 IV 文型] | They asked me 200 dollars for deposit. |

## 2 イタリック部分の群動詞を他の動詞で言い換えなさい.

2.1 go away = leave    2.2 pass away = die    2.3 cut out = stop

2.4 put off = postpone    2.5 fill out = write    2.6 let down = disappoint

2.7 take to = like    2.8 stand by = support    2.9 get A through … = survive …

2.10 look up to = respect    2.11 cut back on = reduce

2.12 be made up of = be formed by

## 3 Oral translation: 以下の日本語を英語にしなさい.

3.1 I will not allow anyone to interfere with my plans.

3.2 Why didn't you text me back soon?

3.3 I suggested that Mary (should) call Ichiro.

3.4 I wish you would come with me.

3.5 That T-shirt looks good on you. Where did you get it?

3.6 When you are hungry, anything tastes good.

3.7 Look out for your health while you are abroad on a trip.

3.8 I have nothing to do with the case. I hate to be asked a lot of questions.

3.9 Recently transportation has become more convenient, and I don't feel it a big bother to go back to my hometown.

3.10 Recycling is not enough to get rid of plastic waste.

3.11 I'm thirsty. Give me something cold to drink.

3.12 She didn't let me go.

3.13 I handed him my business card with my phone number.

## 第2章　時制と相

### 1　次の各文のかっこの中の選択肢の中から，適切な時制・相表現を選びなさい．
1.1　go　　1.2　had been　　1.3　are you doing　　1.4　has been
1.5　I'm not being　　1.6　will be joining　　1.7　was finally　　1.8　have been
1.9　would / headed　　1.10　start　　1.11　I'm　　1.12　asks　　1.13　turned
1.14　have　　1.15　will have traveled　　1.16　had known

### 2　Oral translation: 以下の日本文を英語にしなさい．
2.1　"Is it raining?" "Yes, it's raining a little bit."
2.2　He promised me that he would come at 1:00 today, but he hasn't yet.
2.3　What had you been doing until I came here?
2.4　I can see Mt. Fuji from the window.
2.5　What did you eat for breakfast today?
2.6　I was surprised to find my teacher had already been there when I entered the class-room.
2.7　A large number of tourists visit Nara every year.
2.8　I will have been to Canada five times if I go there next year.
2.9　Communication has become faster since the advent of smartphones.
2.10 The United Nations report warns that climate change will get worse unless appropriate measures are taken.

## 第3章　助動詞

### 1　次の空所（　　）に入る語を選択肢から選びなさい．
1.1　come　　1.2　like　　1.3　rather　　1.4　sure　　1.5　dare

### 2　次の英文を日本語訳しなさい．
2.1　大阪駅の中央コンコースは人でいっぱいで，待ち合わせた人に会えなかった．
2.2　東京に行ったら，プリンスホテルに泊まってもいいね．
2.3　「トイレに行ってもいいですか」「授業が始まる前に行っておくべきだったね」
2.4　経済学を専攻しているならば，少なくとも毎日，新聞を読んで世界の動きについていかなければならない．
2.5　私には君が言ったことは許せない．

## 3 （　　）内の語句を使用して，以下の日本語を英語にしなさい.

3.1　Excuse me, Mr. Takada, but could you spare (me) a minute / moment / little time?

3.2　I'll call on you this evening.

3.3　We [They] don't have (so) much snow in Nara.

3.4　Let's go out [break off] for lunch now.

3.5　I didn't do well on the first semester's exam; I will try to do better in the second semester.


# 第4章　法と仮定法構文

## 1　以下の英文を日本語訳しなさい.

1.1　車が壊れていなかったら，電車に間に合っただろうに.

1.2　都合がいいなら，9時に会いましょう.

1.3　彼が私の息子なら，誇りに思うでしょう.

1.4　流暢に英語を話すことができたらとどれほど思ったことか.

1.5　「郵便局への道を教えてくれませんか」
　　　「この道をまっすぐ行って，2番目の角を曲がるとあります」

## 2　次の空所（　　）内の語句を並び替えて，意味の通る適切な英文にしなさい.

2.1　I would show you how to do it if I knew myself.

2.2　The child would have been killed if the train hadn't stopped quickly.

2.3　If you can type, you ought to be able to get a job.

2.4　If you don't have time this evening, why don't we make a date tomorrow.

2.5　If you cause an accident while you are a student driver, your temporary license will be revoked.

## 3　（　　）内の語句を使って，次の日本語を英語にしなさい.

3.1　I would have gone if I had known.

3.2　If dinner is not ready, I will go without eating it.

3.3　The dog would have bitten you if it had not been tied up.

3.4　I wish the English class would be canceled tomorrow.

3.5　Where would you like to go when you get your driver's license?

## 第5章　話法と時制の一致

### 1　以下の日本語を英語に訳しなさい.
1.1　I am often asked how to get to [the way to] (the) Tokyo Sky Tree.
1.2　I told the taxi driver that he was [we were] going the wrong way.
1.3　He said that his father had been a policeman before.
1.4　A: "What would you like (to eat)?"
　　　B: "I'd like a pizza."
　　　C: "Coffee and a sandwich, please."
　　　D: "Just water is enough for me."
1.5　A: "Why are there so many deer in Nara Park?"
　　　B: "Well, I'm not sure." / "Well, I have no idea."

### 2　以下の英語を日本語に訳しなさい.
2.1　吉田君は,「3ヶ月定期を買ったばかりなのに, 落としてしまった」と嘆いていた.
2.2　駅で, 切符の自動販売機が故障したので, たたいたら, 駅員が「たたかないでください」と言った.
2.3　道路情報によると大阪の外環状線がずいぶん混んでいるらしいよ.
2.4　A: 君はなぜ遅刻したのですか.
　　　B: 電車が京都で故障して30分間動かなかったのです.
2.5　A: 鳥居はなぜ赤く塗ってあるのですか.
　　　B: さあ, 何か宗教的な意味があるのでしょう.
2.6　インフルエンザになったので医者にかかったら, 早く治りたければ, 少なくとも8時間は睡眠をとらなければならないと言われた.
2.7　受験のとき, 普通の鉛筆は良いが, シャープペンシルは使ってはいけないと言われた.
2.8　うちの子供が小学生の頃, 家族でカナダへ旅行した. その子たちは場所の名前を言ってもその場所へ行ったことはほとんど覚えていない.


## 第6章　準動詞

### 1　次の英文を日本語訳しなさい.
1.1　うちの息子は休みだというのに朝からずっと勉強だ. 少しはテニスでもやればいいのに.
1.2　前の日曜日に高校時代の同窓会があってね. 行った甲斐があったよ. 3年ぶりに会っ

た友達とずいぶん話がはずんでね.

1.3 多くの企業は, いわゆる終身雇用制度があるために, 新規採用者は定年までその会社で勤めると思っているのが普通だ.

1.4 近年のアメリカ自動車産業の不況で, たくさんの労働者がクビにされた.

1.5 先生の行った調査では, 生徒の80パーセントは大学進学を希望している.

1.6 野党が弱体なために, 自民党が長い間政権の座にある.

1.7 「日本では選挙権は何歳で与えられるんですか」「18歳です」「アメリカと同じです. 車の運転は16歳からで, ほとんどの州では喫煙・飲酒は21歳からです」

## 2 次の日本語を, ( ) の語句を使用して英語に訳しなさい.

2.1 I have finished preparing for tomorrow's classes.

2.2 When you come across a word (that) you don't know, all you can do is look it up in the dictionary.

2.3 Do you know the old man dozing (off) over there?

2.4 Do you [Would you] mind opening the window?

2.5 He got [had] his leg broken in the accident.

2.6 I enjoy going to see the movies.

2.7 I can smell (the) fish burning.

2.8 "I'd like to subscribe to [take] an English newspaper."

## PART III 品詞を中心として

### 第1章 名詞, 冠詞

## 1 次の文のかっこの中に, a/an, the, 無冠詞 (冠詞なし) のどれかを入れなさい.

(1) a　(2) The　(3) a　(4) an　(5) なし　(6) なし　(7) なし　(8) the　(9) the　(10) a　(11) a　(12) a　(13) なし　(14) The　(15) なし　(16) なし　(17) the

## 2 Oral translation: ( ) の語句を使用して, 以下の日本文を英語にしなさい.

2.1 I bought two pairs of shoes in Osaka yesterday.

2.2 He has been in bed with flu for more than a week.

2.3 Five years is a long time in the world of technology.

2.4 Would you like another cup of tea?

2.5 Which kind of pet is right for me, a cat or a dog?

2.6 My desire is to serve society.

2.7 It is my understanding that there is a three-year warranty on this cell phone.

2.8 You need flour, water, a few slices of pork, finely chopped cabbage and eggs to make okonomiyaki.

2.9 Did you have salad for breakfast? You have tomato on your face.

2.10 My advice is to open your mind for new things and ideas.

2.11 I hear that his family is big and he is the second eldest of his five brothers and sisters.

## 第2章　代名詞

### 1　かっこに適切な代名詞を入れなさい．日本語がある場合はそれを参考にしなさい．

1.1 them　　1.2 each　　1.3 its　　1.4 They　　1.5 Both　　1.6 those　　1.7 himself
1.8 his/nothing　　1.9 her

### 2　Oral translation: （　　）内の語句を利用して，日本文を英語にしなさい．

2.1 I don't need red shoes. Can I see those black ones?

2.2 Friends should trust each other.

2.3 I have nothing to hide.

2.4 What do you want me to do?

2.5 A new study finds that the laughing patterns of human babies are similar to those of another species.

2.6 My mother was waiting for me on her way back home.

2.7 None of us expected this would happen.

2.8 Some coffee lovers tweet something about coffee they drink every day.

2.9 He spent more than half of his life in New York, and it was full of happiness.

2.10 It is not easy for me to build that sort of business she did.

## 第3章　形容詞と限定詞

### 1　形容詞型 It is Adj. that, NP be Adj. that, It is Adj. to do, NP is Adj. to do, NP is Adj. PrepP を活用して自由に英作しなさい．

自由解答

## 2 以下の英文で使用されている形容詞（beautiful, honest）は，一時性もしくは永続性のどちらか述べなさい．

(1) は両方とも一時性形容詞．　　(2a) は一時性形容詞，(2b) は永続性形容詞．

## 3 Oral translation: （　　）内の語句を使用して英語にしなさい．

3.1　That is too difficult for a three-year-old child to understand.

3.2　Next typhoon will surely hit [strike] the Kii Peninsula./I am sure that next typhoon will hit the Kii Peninsula.

3.3　It is surprising [a surprise] that he failed [should have failed] the Principles of Economic course.

3.4　We are in trouble because our father is too difficult to handle.

3.5　It is impossible for me to swim ten kilometers./I cannot swim ten kilometers (no matter what).

3.6　You were wise to turn [have turned] off the gas right after the earthquake occurred [happened]./It was wise of you to turn off the gas right after the earthquake occurred [happened].

3.7　It is comforting to see beautiful flowers./Beautiful flowers are comforting to see./The sight of beautiful flowers gives us comfort.

3.8　I haven't played tennis for a while. I now feel really eager [anxious] to play.

## 第4章　副詞と副詞的語句

## 1 I'm very tired. と I'm tired a lot. の意味の違いを説明しなさい．

I'm very tired. は「とても疲れた」いう意味で，very が形容詞の意味を強めている．それに対して，I'm tired a lot. は「よく疲れる」という意味で，疲れることの多さを述べている．

## 2 以下の英文の違いを説明しなさい．

(1) a.　I slept until nine.

b.　I didn't sleep until nine.

(2) a.　I stayed there until nine.

b.　I didn't stay there until nine.

(1a) は「9時まで寝ていた」，(1b) は「9時までは寝なかった」（=9時過ぎに寝た）という意味で，(1b) は寝ている状態の始まりの時が否定されている．

(2) の場合，(2a) は「9時までそこに滞在していた」，(2b) は「9時にはそこを離れていた」（=9時までいたわけではない）という意味で，滞在の終わりの時が否定されている．

## 3 確信の度合いを表す副詞，頻度副詞を利用して，自身の行動を英作しなさい.
自由解答

## 4 Oral translation: (    ) 内の語句を使用して英語にしなさい.

4.1 I want only orange juice.

4.2 Henry text-messaged me a little while ago.

4.3 I will come to [get to/arrive at] Shin-Osaka Station by Shinkansen. Come and meet me there.

4.4 The door opened a little [a fraction of an inch] and a cat came in.

4.5 I am sorry I was sick and I couldn't come to [attend] the meeting the other day.

4.6 I usually play tennis on Sunday mornings.

4.7 I visited Professor Yamada's office without an appointment, but luckily he was in his office.

4.8 I got [received] a book from my friend [a friend of mine] in U.S. after waiting a long time.

4.9 My idea [What I am thinking] is quite different from yours [what you are thinking].

4.10 I never drink and drive.

## 第5章　比較

## 1 以下の同等比較のフレーズを利用して，自由に英作しなさい.
自由解答

## 2 The book is more interesting than any other book I have ever read. を，(1) such を使用した同等比較の英文，(2) 最上級を使用した英文に書き換えなさい.

(1)　I have never read such an interesting book as this.

(2)　The book is the most interesting of all the books I have ever read.

## 3 フレーズ as good as it gets が使用された This is as good as it gets. の意味を述べなさい.

これ以上良くなる見込みが（少しも）ない.

解説：この意味には，(1) ここまで来られて最高.　(2) ここまで来られただけで十分.　(3) ここまで来られたけれど，これ以上はどうにもならない，という3つの評価のいずれかを含んでおり，その評価は文脈によって異なる.

## 4 Oral translation: ( ) 内の語句を使用して英語にしなさい.
4.1 Which do you like better, spring or fall?

4.2 Usain Bolt is the fastest in the hundred-meter dash so far.

4.3 The Chinese cuisine I ate today was as good as that which I ate in Chinatown the other day.

4.4 When I saw Loch Ness, I felt I had never seen such a beautiful lake before.

4.5 Do you know who the former president of the United States is?

4.6 Portland, Oregon is said to be one of the most beautiful cities in the U.S.

4.7 The personal computer is as good as new.

4.8 This cake is not half as delicious as it looks.

4.9 I'm running out of time, I can't wait any longer.

4.10 I misunderstood that he should know better.


## 第6章 関係詞と疑問詞

## 1 以下の2つの文を, 適切な関係詞を使用して1つの文にしなさい.
a. She has a brother, who is now in London.

b. This is the house, where Washington was born.

c. She asked friends whose opinion she respected.


## 2 以下の2つの例文を, [ ] 内の指示に従い書き換えなさい.
a. Is this exactly *what* he said? [that which]  →  Is this exactly that which he said?

b. To *whom* do you wish to talk? [who]  →  Who do you wish to talk to?


## 3 関係副詞 where, when, how, why, whenever, wherever を使用して, 自由に英作しなさい.
自由解答


## 4 Oral translation: ( ) 内の語句を使用して英語にしなさい.
4.1 She / He is the person who called on you this morning.

4.2 Minako, who was born in U.S., has difficulty getting adjusted to the Japanese way of life.

4.3 I fell in love with a girl when I was a high school student, but now I can't even remember her name.

4.4 This book, which everyone wants to have, is out of print.

4.5 Okinawa is the place (that) everyone wants [would like] to visit in summer at least

once.
4.6  A: What would you like for your birthday present?
     B: I would like flowers; any flowers would be fine.
4.7  This is the reason I quit my job.
4.8  He is a graduate of what is known as a prestigious university, which fact does not guarantee his successful future.
4.9  There once was a foreigner who, when he saw apartment houses in Japan, said that Japanese people live in rabbit hutches.
4.10 What is called a 'mansion' in Japan is actually 'an apartment house / a flat' or 'condominium' in English. A 'mansion' is a grand building built on a large estate in English usage.


## 第 7 章　接続詞・前置詞

### 1　各文のかっこに接続詞を入れなさい．日本語がある場合は日本語を参考にしなさい．
(1) as　　(2) because　　(3) in case　　(4) before　　(5) if

### 2　各文のかっこに前置詞を入れなさい．日本語がある場合は日本語を参考にしなさい．
(1) in / in　　(2) with　　(3) of　　(4) after　　(5) at / of　　(6) through　　(7) in
(8) during または in　　(9) for / about　　(10) in / by

### 3　Oral translation: (　　) 内の語句を使用して英語にしなさい．
3.1  I just nodded and didn't say anything else.
3.2  If you stick to the schedule, I may have to drop everything I'm doing now.
3.3  A man in his thirties came out, and I thought he is the person I have been looking for.
3.4  About an hour after my father had gone downstairs, I heard him shout, "Dinner is ready."
3.5  I'm not sure whether he plays baseball, but I'm sure he runs marathons.
3.6  He said that the furniture there was from Ikea.
3.7  Eric started a rumor about me and told everyone at school that I was seeing Mary.
3.8  "What are you doing here?" "I was out for a ride on my bike."
3.9  I had been out of breath by the time I got to the park.
3.10 Though I knew exactly who he meant, I asked, "Who?"

# 索　引

1. 「用語」と「語彙」に分け，アルファベット順に並べた.
2. 数字はページ数を示し，これに続く〜は次ページ（以降）に続くことを示す.

## 用　語

239

【監修者・著者紹介】

**八木 克正** (やぎ かつまさ)
関西学院大学名誉教授．専門は英語の語法・文法，辞書学，フレイジオロジー．
主要業績：『英語定型表現研究』（共著，開拓社，2013），『熟語本位英和中辞典 新版』（校注，岩波書店，2016），『斎藤さんの英和中辞典──響きあう日本語と英語を求めて』（岩波書店，2016），『英語にまつわるエトセトラ』（研究社，2018），『現代高等英文法──学習文法から科学文法へ』（開拓社，2021）など．

**井上 亜依** (いのうえ あい)
東洋大学経済学部教授．専門は現代英語のフレイジオロジー（定型表現研究），英語辞書学．
主要業績：『英語定型表現研究の体系化を目指して──形態論・意味論・音響音声学の視点から』（研究社，2018［2019年日本英語コミュニケーション学会学会賞受賞］），『英語のフレーズ研究への誘い』（開拓社，2019），『フレーズ活用英語塾：世界で活躍できる人材になる』（小学館，2019），など．

**住吉 誠** (すみよし まこと)
関西学院大学経済学部教授．専門は英語語法文法，フレイジオロジー，辞書学．
主要業績：『小学館 オックスフォード 英語コロケーション辞典』（編集委員，小学館，2015），『談話のことば2 規範からの解放』（研究社，2016），『慣用表現・変則的表現から見える英語の姿』（編著，開拓社，2019），『コーパス研究の展望』（共著，開拓社，2020），など．

**藏薗 和也** (くらぞの かずや)
神戸学院大学人文学部講師．専門は英語の語法・文法，シノニム比較，コロケーション．
主要業績：「起動動詞 get, fall, set に後続する統語形式 to V, V-ing 及び補文動詞の選択基準」（『日本英語コミュニケーション学会紀要』，第25巻第1号，1-15，2016），「起動動詞 begin と start に後続する to 不定詞及び動名詞構文の性質」（『英語語法文法研究』，第23号，102-117，2016），「to 不定詞補文及び動名詞補文における選択制限──起動動詞 grow, proceed, commence, resume を例に」（『日本英語コミュニケーション学会紀要』，第28巻第1号，1-15，2019），など．

## 文法活用の大学英語演習
(*Grammar-based English Practice for College Students*)

| | |
|---|---|
| 監修者 | 八木克正 |
| 著　者 | 井上亜依・住吉誠・藏薗和也 |
| 発行者 | 武村哲司 |
| 印刷所 | 日之出印刷株式会社 |

2022 年 12 月 12 日　第 1 版第 1 刷発行©

発行所　　　株式会社　開 拓 社

〒 112-0013 東京都文京区音羽 1-22-16
電話　（03）5395-7101（代表）
振替　00160-8-39587
http://www.kaitakusha.co.jp

ISBN978-4-7589-2379-8　C3082